Cricket

Cricket

A Nation's Passion and Progress

Rafel Mechlore

Leader Enterprises

CONTENTS

INDEX

Introduction

1. The significance of cricket in various nations
2. Overview of the book's purpose and scope
3. Brief history of cricket and its global appeal
4. Thesis statement: Exploring the deep-rooted passion for cricket and its impact on the progress of nations.

Chapter 1: The Birth of Cricket
1.1 The origins of cricket in England
1.2 Early rules and development of the game
1.3 The spread of cricket to other nations

Chapter 2: Cricket and National Identity
2.1 Cricket's role in shaping national identity
2.2 Iconic cricketing moments that united nations
2.3 How cricket reflects cultural values and norms

Chapter 3: Passion for the Game
3.1 Cricket as a religion in some nations
3.2 The fervor of cricket fans
3.3 The role of cricket in social bonding

Chapter 4: Cricket and Politics
4.1 The intersection of cricket and politics
4.2 How cricket has been used for diplomatic purposes
4.3 Controversies and political influences on the game

Chapter 5: Cricket and Gender

5.1 Women's cricket and its growth

5.2 Gender dynamics within cricket

5.3 The changing landscape of women's participation in the sport

Chapter 6: Cricket and Development

6.1 The economic impact of cricket

6.2 Development of infrastructure and facilities

6.3 The role of cricket in education and youth development

Chapter 7: The Modern Era

7.1 The impact of technology on the game

7.2 Evolution of formats: Test, One Day, and T20

7.3 The rise of franchise leagues and their influence

Chapter 8: Global Tensions and Diplomacy through Cricket

8.1 Cricket as a diplomatic tool in international relations

8.2 High-profile series and their geopolitical significance

8.3 The power of cricket in fostering international cooperation

Chapter 9: Challenges and Controversies

9.1 Match-fixing and corruption

9.2 Issues related to governance and administration

9.3 The struggle for inclusion and diversity

Chapter 10: Cricket's Future

10.1 The potential for further globalization

10.2 The impact of climate change on cricket

10.3 The evolving fan experience and technological advancements

INTRODUCTION

The book "Cricket: A Nation's Passion and Progress" takes the reader on an epic adventure through the fascinating world of one of the most popular sports in the world. This book is a witness to the deep-seated enthusiasm that cricket arouses in the hearts of millions of people and to the significant impact that it has on the advancement of nations. It is a celebration of a game that crosses borders, countries, and backgrounds, connecting people in their shared love for this sport that has been around for hundreds of years.

Cricket has a long history of being admired as a sport that upholds a unique set of values and customs. Cricket was once a quaint game in England, but it has since blossomed into a worldwide sensation. Its origins may be traced back to the 16th century. The fact that it has made its way across multiple countries and civilizations is evidence of its malleability and widespread appeal. Cricket has evolved over the years to become more than just a game; it has knitted itself into the fabric of national identities and cultural landscapes, and as a result, it is now an essential component of the collective consciousness of many countries.

This book aims to expose the complex nature of cricket, including its rich history, its capacity to shape and express national identities, its potential to create progress on multiple fronts, and its promise as a force that transcends borders and brings people together. Specifically, the book will focus on how cricket has the ability to shape and express national identities. In the following pages, we shall investigate the history of cricket, beginning with its rudimentary beginnings and ending with its current status as a global spectacle.

Fans all over the world see cricket not only as a sporting event, as it is commonly known, but also as an emotional trip. It possesses the capacity to arouse ardor, elation, and even occasional grief in its audience. The roars of the stadium, the intense support of the fans, and the brilliant performances that have been carved into the annals of cricketing history all contribute to the aura of mystery that surrounds this sport. As we delve deeper into this story, we will come across instances of sports brilliance, incredible camaraderie among fans, and the actualization of dreams, all of which are connected by a shared passion for cricket.

However, the significance of cricket extends well beyond the playing field. The sport has been a significant factor in the development of the political landscape of nations, an influential force in the practice of diplomacy, and a potent instrument for the advancement of international relations. It is an example of how something as seemingly simple as a game can have far-reaching implications that extend beyond the boundary ropes, and it has the power to bring nations together as well as sometimes split them.

In addition, "Cricket: A Nation's Passion and Progress" investigates the game's altering connection with gender by digging into the meteoric ascent of women's cricket and the shifting dynamics that are occurring inside the sport. This article investigates the role that cricket has played in the economic progress of countries, particularly in terms of fostering the expansion of infrastructure and creating employment possibilities. The author also explores the manner in which the sport of cricket has evolved into an important part of the educational system and the growth of young people.

A new epoch in the history of cricket has begun with the arrival of the contemporary period. This new phase is distinguished by the introduction of new technologies, the development of a variety of formats, and the rise of franchise leagues. The sport and the way it has an effect on societies have both been refashioned as a result of these advancements. We will investigate the ways in which technology has improved the fan experience, making it more immersive and involved than it has ever been, as well as the ways in which cricket leagues such as the Indian Premier League (IPL) have become global sporting phenomena that transcend national lines.

Cricket is more than simply a game; it is also a tool for diplomacy, a catalyst for social change, an economic driver, and a mirror that reflects the ideals and goals of the nations it comes into contact with. However, it is also confronted with a large number of difficulties, including scandals involving match-fixing, problems with governance, and the battle to be inclusive and diverse. This book will dive into these concerns and present a thorough assessment of the obstacles that cricket must overcome in order to continue to be a force for positive change in the world.

As we get to the end of this journey, we will take some time to consider the future of cricket. We will think about the sport's ability to continue its spread across the world, its flexibility in the face of environmental concerns, and the role it will play as technology continues to advance. A call to action will urge readers to acknowledge and support the significant impact that cricket has had over the ages, and the everlasting value of the game will be reiterated in the piece.

The book "Cricket: A Nation's Passion and Progress" is an in-depth investigation of the impact that cricket has had on nations, beginning with its humble beginnings and progressing all the way up to its current standing as a phenomenon that spans the entire planet. It is required reading for anybody interested in the profound connections that exist between sports, culture, politics, and the advancement of society. Cricket fans and sports fans in general will find this book fascinating. This book provides a thorough assessment of the significant influence that cricket has had on the world and emphasizes its function as more than just a sport; rather, it is a source of national pride, unity, and advancement.

1. The significance of cricket in various nations

Cricket, which is frequently referred to as a "gentleman's game," carries a special meaning that is quite significant in many countries all over the world. It is a cultural phenomenon, a source of national pride, and a mirror reflecting the ideals and aspirations of the nations that it affects. It is more than just a sport. This essay dives into the relevance of cricket in a variety of countries, examining how the sport has become ingrained in their culture and examining the meaning of the game for those who participate in it as well as those who watch it.

1. **The sport of cricket in India**
   In India, playing cricket is more than simply a pastime—it's a way of life. The passion that the Indian people have for cricket is unrivaled, especially considering the country's population of nearly 1.3 billion people. The Indian Premier League (IPL) has evolved into a worldwide phenomenon in the world of sports, luring the best players in the world as well as massive viewers all over the world. The sport is able to transcend geographic and language boundaries, which helps to unite an otherwise diverse society. Cricket matches have the ability to bring an entire nation to a complete standstill, and cricketing greats such as Sachin Tendulkar and Virat Kohli are worshiped as if they were gods. Many people consider cricket to be more than just a game; rather, it is an essential component of who they are, and their accomplishments in the sport are a tremendous source of pride for them.

2. **Cricket in the land Down Under**
   Cricket is more than just a sport to the people of Australia; it's a way of life. Pride and honor are represented by the Baggy Green, which is worn by Australian cricketers competing in Test matches. The game of cricket has been crucial in the formation of the Australian national identity. The competition for the ashes with England is a historic and emotional one that extends beyond the boundary lines. It is well known that Australian cricketers are renowned for their tenacity, toughness, and never-give-up mentality. Cricket is a sport that holds a very unique place in the hearts of Australians, and cricketing greats such as Don Bradman and Shane Warne are venerated as national idols.

3. **Cricket in the United Kingdom**
   The history of cricket can be traced back to England, and even now, the game continues to carry an enormous amount of weight in the country. The sport of cricket has strong ties to both the traditions and the summers of England.

In the history of the sport, legendary locations such as Lord's and The Oval have played host to important moments. Fans of English cricket are recognized for their steadfast support, especially when the sport is going through difficult times, and the Ashes rivalry with Australia is a source of national pride for the country. Cricket in England is a symbol of a connection to the past as well as a profound affection for the tradition and principles that underpin the sport.

4. **The sport of cricket played in the West Indies**

   Cricket is more than just a sport in the West Indies; it serves as a unifying force for the region, which comprises many different nations and cultures. The West Indies cricket team, also known as the "Windies," has been seen as a sign of tenacity and cohesion throughout the region. Because it transcends political and socioeconomic differences, the sport has been essential in bringing together a number of Caribbean nations, including Jamaica, Trinidad & Tobago, Barbados, and others. Not only are cricket greats such as Vivian Richards and Brian Lara cultural icons, but they are also sporting superstars in their own right. The sport of cricket in the West Indies instills a sense of national pride and serves as a motivational force for many people.

5. **Cricket in the country of Pakistan**

   The Pakistani people have a deep and abiding love for the sport of cricket. The sport has brought brief periods of elation and festivity to a country that must frequently contend with a variety of difficulties. Cricketing greats like Imran Khan and Wasim Akram have emerged from Pakistan in spite of the country's troubled history and current security situation. The sport brings together individuals from a variety of provinces, languages, and cultural backgrounds. Cricket is a wellspring of optimism and national pride for Pakistanis, and the hosting of international matches on Pakistani soil is viewed as a metaphor for the country's resiliency and prosperity.

6. **Cricket in the country of South Africa**

   The sport of cricket in South Africa is a reflection of the nation's complicated history as well as its journey towards reconciliation and harmony. The sport was instrumental in the overthrow of the apartheid regime, and the cohesiveness of the national cricket team, often known as the Proteas, became a symbol of optimism and progress at this time. The likes of Nelson Mandela and Hansie Cronje are examples of players who have made an indelible mark on the sport's relevance in the country. Cricket in South Africa is both a symbol of the nation's dedication to diversity and a reminder of the country's progress toward becoming a society that is more welcoming to all.

7. **Cracking in the Land of the Lankans**

   Cricket is more than just a sport in Sri Lanka; it is also a source of national pride and solidarity for the entire country. It is a credit to Sri Lanka's resiliency and dedication that the country's cricket team was able to go from being an underdog to winning the Cricket World Cup in 1996, despite the odds being stacked against them. Cricket tournaments frequently act as a unifying force, bringing together people from a variety of cultural and racial backgrounds. Iconic players such as Muttiah Muralitharan and Kumar Sangakkara are beloved personalities in the sport, and cricket matches are also known to do so. In Sri Lanka, cricket is a symbol of both the nation's spirit and its hopes for the future.

8. **Cricket in the Bangladeshi Countryside**

Cricket in Bangladesh has shown substantial expansion and has emerged as a major source of the country's great sense of national pride. The nation has gained prominence on a global scale as a result of the sport, and the passion that people have for the game has brought them together. It was a momentous occasion when Bangladesh defeated Pakistan in the Cricket World Cup in 1999; as a result, individuals like Shakib Al Hasan and Tamim Iqbal have been elevated to the status of national heroes. Cricket in Bangladesh is emblematic of the nation's march toward growth and its dedication to performing admirably on the international scene.

9. **Cricket in the Afghani Countryside**

The history of cricket in Afghanistan is one of perseverance and optimism. The young people of Afghanistan now have a conduit through which they may channel their ambitions and energies thanks to the sport. The success of the Afghanistan national cricket team in international competition is evidence of the tenacity of the country as a whole. Players such as Rashid Khan and Mohammad Nabi have not only been successful in the game, but they have also become icons of national pride due to their accomplishments. Cricket in Afghanistan symbolizes the nation's journey for recognition and achievement, as well as the progress that has been made along that path.

10. **The national sport of New Zealand, cricket**

Cricket, which is played in New Zealand, is strongly embedded in the culture of the country, and it serves as a reflection of the nation's commitment to sportsmanship and fair play. The New Zealand national cricket team, known as the Blackcaps, has earned a reputation for being fiercely competitive and having a high regard for the sport. Cricket matches, particularly those played against Australia and England, have a special place in the hearts of New Zealanders. Players such as Sir Richard Hadlee and Brendon McCullum are revered names in the sport, and New Zealanders look forward to these encounters with great anticipation. In New Zealand, cricket exemplifies the nation's commitment to honesty and fair play in athletic competition.

B. Overview of the book's purpose and scope

The book "Cricket: A Nation's Passion and Progress" is an in-depth investigation into the significant influence that cricket has had on the countries that have embraced the sport. This book aims to shed light on the many facets of cricket, from its historical roots to its contemporary impact on society, culture, politics, and economic growth. Topics covered include the history of cricket, its origins, and its evolution. The purpose of this summary is to provide insight into the primary ideas of the book, as well as its objectives and the scope of the issues that are discussed inside its pages.

1. **The Reason for Writing the Book**

   The book "Cricket: A Nation's Passion and Progress" has been written with the primary intention of shedding light on the amazing part that cricket plays in the formation of national identities as well as the progress of nations. Although cricket is most commonly thought of as a sport, the game is, in reality, a dynamic force that extends significantly beyond than the boundary ropes. This book serves as a witness to the deep-seated enthusiasm that the sport of cricket sparks in the hearts of millions of people and its power to move nations forward.

   The purpose of this project is to track the historical development of cricket, beginning with its inception in England and ending with the sport's widespread popularity around the world, with an emphasis on illuminating the seminal events that have played a significant role in molding cricket's trajectory. In order to demonstrate how cricket has become an essential component of national identity, which reflects cultural values, traditions, and aspirations while also unifying disparate populations, the goal of this project is to demonstrate how cricket has become an integral component of national identity.

   Exploring the great Passion That Cricket Inspires in Its Fans: The goal of this project is to investigate the great passion that cricket elicits in its followers by diving into the feelings, rituals, and steadfast commitment that make cricket more than just a game.

   Discovering how cricket has been used as a diplomatic tool and analyzing the sport's place in the context of international relations are some of the topics that will be covered in this section. Political and diplomatic significance will also be discussed.

   Gender Dynamics: The goal of this section is to investigate the shifting dynamics of gender in cricket, with a specific focus on the expansion of women's cricket and the changing roles that women play in the sport.

   An examination of the economic impact of cricket, including its part in the process of constructing infrastructure, producing job opportunities, and fostering growth in nations is the goal of this development project.

   The Modern Era and Technological Developments: The goal of this section is to investigate the impact that technology has had on the game of cricket, the development of cricket forms over time, and the rise of franchise leagues in the modern landscape of cricket.

   Demonstrating How Cricket Can Be Both a Source of Global Tension and a

Tool for Diplomacy The purpose of this section is to illustrate how cricket can be both a source of global tension and a tool for diplomacy, with high-profile series carrying geopolitical relevance.

To address the challenges and controversies that the sport of cricket is currently confronted with, such as match-fixing, governance issues, and the continual fight for inclusivity and diversity.

Consider the future of cricket, including its potential for increased globalization, its ability to adapt to climate change, and its developing position in the increasingly digital era.

2. The Subject Matter of the Book

The author digs into the early beginnings of cricket in England, as well as the growth of the game and its expansion to many regions of the world, in this book that offers a historical perspective.

It explains how cricket molds and reflects national identity, values, and cultural norms, uniting people with a shared love for the sport. Cricket also brings people together because of their shared love of the sport.

Emotions, Rituals, and Customs: This book examines the strong love and steadfast allegiance that cricket fans have for the game, as well as the customs, rituals, and feelings that are linked with it.

It examines the ways in which cricket connects with politics, diplomacy, and international relations, especially high-profile series that have political significance. Another topic it covers is the diplomatic and political dimensions of cricket.

This book investigates the shifting environment of women's cricket as well as the gender dynamics that exist within the sport, including the empowerment of female cricket players. Gender Dynamics.

It investigates the economic impact of cricket, with a particular emphasis on the expansion of cricket-related enterprises and job possibilities, as well as the development of infrastructure.

The Modern Era and Technology: This section of the book examines the impact that technology has had on the game, the development of several formats (Test, One Day, and T20), and the advent of franchise leagues such as the Indian Premier League.

It investigates how cricket can be both a source of global tension and a diplomatic tool, providing examples of cricket's function in forging international collaboration. "Global Tensions and Diplomacy"

Challenges and Controversies: This book discusses a wide range of cricket's challenges and controversies, such as match-fixing, governance issues, and initiatives to encourage inclusiveness and diversity.

It takes into account the possibility for increased globalization of the sport, the influence that climate change will have on cricket, as well as the changing nature of the fan experience in the digital age.

This book covers not only cricket as a game, but also cricket as a cultural, political, and economic force. It is not confined to just covering cricket as a game. It incorporates historical narratives, personal anecdotes, as well as a forward-looking perspective of cricket's enduring significance in the nations that it touches.

C. Brief history of cricket and its global appeal

Cricket, a sport with a long history and traditions that run deep, has developed into a worldwide sensation that defies cultural, geographical, and linguistic barriers. This essay offers a concise summary of the historical beginnings of cricket, its development into a sport played all over the world, and the elements that have contributed to the sport's continued popularity on a worldwide scale.

1. Initial Beginnings and Early Development

   The sixteenth century in England is considered to be the birthplace of cricket. The game probably descended from earlier sports involving a bat and a ball that were played in the nation. Some of the earliest mentions of cricket may be discovered in historical documents, such as a court case that took place in 1598 and concerned a little boy who was injured by a cricket ball. By the 17th century, cricket had established a following in the more rural parts of England in the United Kingdom.

   The evolution of cricket throughout the 18th century had a significant impact on the game's regulations as well as its structure in the current day. The Hambledon Club, which was established in the late 1700s, was an important contributor to the process of standardizing the rules. In 1788, the Marylebone Cricket Club (also known as the MCC) published what is now known as the Laws of Cricket, which serve as the primary regulatory document for the cricket sport.

2. The Initial Propagation of the Game

   The growth of the British Empire in the 19th century was a significant factor in the dispersal of cricket throughout the rest of the world. The game was brought to a number of different regions by British colonists and military personnel. These regions included the Indian subcontinent, the Caribbean, Australia, South Africa, and New Zealand. The game of cricket got deeply ingrained in the culture of these territories almost immediately after it was introduced there.

3. The Origins of Global Cricket

   When a team of Indigenous Australians traveled to England in 1844, it was there that the first ever international cricket match took place. This event is considered to be the commencement of international cricket and paved the basis for subsequent international competitions. At the Melbourne Cricket Ground in 1877, the first-ever Test match was played, which established the Test format as the longest format of the game. The match was played between Australia and England. The term "Test cricket" refers to competitions that are played between countries at the highest possible level.

4. The Game's Appeal to the World at Large

1. The One-of-a-Kind Quality of the Game:

   Cricket is an unusual sport because it combines elements of strategy, talent, and agility. Cricket is played in a variety of formats, including Test matches, One Day Internationals (ODIs), and Twenty20 (T20) matches, each of which is designed to appeal to a distinct audience and showcase a unique playing style. This variety helps to the game's broad appeal due to its many different aspects.

2. Importance to Cultural Traditions:

   The game of cricket has been deeply ingrained in the culture and history of many countries throughout the world where it is played. As a source of national pride, it is a reflection of the nations' morals and customs, making it an important cultural artifact.

3. Rivalries on the International Stage:

   Fans from all around the world are captivated by iconic rivalries such as the Ashes series that is played between England and Australia and the contests that take place between India and Pakistan. These competitions transcend the realm of sports and take on a significance all their own, both culturally and historically.

4. Icons of the Sporting World:

   The sport of cricket has spawned legendary figures who are revered not only for their on-field

   success but also for the contributions they have made to the countries in which they have played. Throughout the history of sport, figures such as Sir Don Bradman, Sir Vivian Richards, Sachin Tendulkar, and Sir Garfield Sobers have attained a place of veneration as icons.

5. Competitive Environment of a High Quality

   The level of play in international cricket is at an all-time high thanks to the fact that countries are fielding excellent and formidable squads. Because of the high level of competition, every cricket match is guaranteed to be exciting and surprising.

6. The Changing Nature of Formats:

   The creation of shorter forms such as one-day internationals and Twenty20 competitions has made the sport more approachable and interesting to a wider audience. These formats, which are distinguished by having matches that go for a shorter amount of time, have drawn fans who may not have the time to watch traditional Test matches.

7. Progresses made in technological areas:

   The overall experience for viewers has been improved thanks to developments in technology such as the Hawk-Eye system for decision reviews and live streaming.

Fans may now have a more immersive experience by following matches in real time and receiving in-depth analysis of the action.

8. The International Spread of Cricket:
   The International Cricket Council (ICC) has been instrumental in the development of the sport and in the administration of its rules and regulations at the global level. As a result of its efforts to globalize the game, new countries like Afghanistan and Ireland have been granted Test status, which has resulted in an expansion of cricket's reach.

9. Including people from different backgrounds:
   The sport of cricket has made significant progress toward fostering an inclusive and diverse environment.
   The commitment of cricket to increasing the sport's appeal has been seen by the expansion of women's cricket as well as the emergence of players from a varied range of backgrounds.

10. Intercultural Communication:

The fact that cricket is played all over the world encourages the sharing of different cultures and strengthens diplomatic ties. Cricket matches are frequently used as a forum for international diplomacy and the development of people-to-people ties between countries.

V. The Growth of Cricket Around the World

The widespread popularity of cricket has contributed to its growth in countries that were not

traditionally considered cricket-playing nations. In international cricket, countries such as Afghanistan and Ireland have made major progress, attaining Test status and becoming competitive at the top level. In addition, international competitions such as the ICC Cricket World Cup and the ICC Twenty20 World Cup highlight the variety of cricket-playing nations from all over the world, as well as their considerable potential.

As a result of the proliferation of franchise-based Twenty20 leagues, such as the Indian Premier League (IPL) and the Big Bash League (BBL), international players are now able to compete against one another, which further contributes to the globalization of cricket as a sport. These competitions feature players from a variety of countries, contributing to cricket's status as a genuinely international phenomenon.

The widespread popularity of cricket can be attributed to the exceptional blend of history, culture, and athletic prowess that characterizes the sport. Cricket is now a worldwide obsession, crossing national boundaries and bringing people from different countries together in a common love for the sport. The game's humble beginnings can be traced back to England. Its sustained success and significance on the world stage can be attributed, in part, to its adaptability to changing times, the evolution of forms, and its commitment to inclusivity and diversity. Cricket is a fascinating example of how a sport can bring people together, celebrate diversity, and win the hearts of millions of people all over the world, and it continues to be played today.

D. Thesis statement: Exploring the deep-rooted passion for cricket and its impact on the progress of nations

Cricket, which is frequently referred to as a sport, is far more than just a game in numerous regions all over the planet. It is a source of deep effect on the development of nations as well as a way of life, a passion for many people. The passion of cricket extends beyond borders, brings together people of varying backgrounds, and is an essential component in the formation of national identities. This essay investigates the deep-seated enthusiasm for cricket and its influence on the development of nations.

It delves into the cultural, social, political, and economic components that make cricket more than just a sport. Ultimately, the essay concludes that cricket is an important factor in the advancement of nations.

1. **Cricket's Role as a Significant Cultural Force**

   The sport of cricket has been deeply ingrained in the culture of a number of different countries. The sport is able to represent cultural values, customs, and aspirations while also reinforcing those values and those traditions. Cricket matches are often linked with local traditions and customs, which elevates them to prominent events on the cultural calendar.

   Cricket is more than just a sport in India; it's also a cultural fixation with the country. During crucial matches, the entire country comes to a complete stop, with millions of fans glued to their TVs or cramming themselves into stadiums. Cricket is a topic of conversation at get-togethers of extended family members, a source of pride and identity, and a force that brings people together in a culture that is diverse and complex.

   In a similar vein, cricket in the West Indies bridges the political and cultural divides that exist there, bringing together individuals from a variety of islands and cultures. It is a reflection of the cultural character of the region, and players such as Sir Vivian Richards are recognized as cultural icons as a result of it.

   Cricket in England has a strong connection to the country's long-standing customs and the warm weather of the summer. Historic events have taken place at iconic locations such as Lord's and The Oval, which have become emblems of national heritage as a result. The competition known as "The Ashes" played between England and Australia is more than just a sport; it is also an important cultural institution.

   These examples illustrate how cricket has been deeply ingrained in the cultural fabric of nations, helping to cultivate a profound sense of belonging and a shared identity in the process.

2. **Bringing Together Various Populations**

   The capacity of cricket to bring together people of different backgrounds can be seen in places like Australia, where the sport is seen as a representation of national pride. Cricket players in Australia are held up as models of the country's grit and determination because of their reputations for being tough and resilient.

Cricket was a significant force in South Africa's struggle against the system of apartheid, which it helped to overthrow. The cohesiveness of the national cricket team, sometimes known as the Proteas, became a symbol of transformation and hope for the country. Players who made significant contributions to the nation's movement toward peace and unity, such as Nelson Mandela and Hansie Cronje, are remembered fondly today.

Cricket brings moments of happiness and celebration to Pakistan, a nation that frequently struggles with a variety of issues. It brings together people from a variety of regions, linguistic groups, and cultural backgrounds. The sport is a source of hope and national pride, and the hosting of international matches on home soil is viewed as a symbol of resiliency and growth in the country.

Cricket in Bangladesh has shown substantial expansion and has emerged as a major source of the country's great sense of national pride. The nation has gained prominence on a global scale as a result of the sport, and the passion that people have for the game has brought them together.

These examples illustrate how cricket can serve as a unifying factor, bringing people together across divisions and contributing to a feeling of national cohesiveness. It brings together people from all sorts of different backgrounds and gives a forum for communal celebrations as well as the sharing of experiences that people have had in common.

3. **The Impact of Cricket on Politics and Policy**

Politics can certainly have an effect on cricket; the sport is not immune to this. Cricket has served as both a medium for international diplomacy and an indicator of the political climate in a number of different countries on several occasions. Matches played on a global stage frequently act as forums for diplomatic exchanges and are crucial in the development of international relations.

The politically charged nature of the cricket match between India and Pakistan is a perfect illustration of the sport's political underpinnings. When two countries compete against one another in a sport, the results are more than just a sports event; they are frequently used as a gauge for how diplomatic relations are doing. Cricket diplomacy, sometimes known as "cricket diplomacy," has been utilized to help alleviate tensions between the two countries and start a dialogue between them.

Cricket has also been used as a tool to promote diplomatic relations between different countries.

There has been geopolitical significance attached to high-profile series like the Ashes and India's tours of Australia in recent years. They facilitate chances for diplomatic encounters and contribute to the strengthening of diplomatic ties between the states who take part.

On the other hand, cricket has also been the subject of controversies concerning politics. As a result of political disagreements, there have been instances of cricketing tie boycotts, punishments, and bans. The fact that political actions can have an effect on cricket serves as a reminder of how sensitive the sport is to the dynamics of geopolitics.

4. **The Affect on the Economy and Its Development**

Cricket is an important part of national and international development, as it helps to generate employment opportunities and contributes to the expansion of nations' economies. The sport is a huge economic force since it has the ability to produce income in the form of broadcasting rights, sponsorships, and advertising.

Cricket-related industries in Australia are responsible for the maintenance of a significant number of jobs and make a contribution to the country's economy. The Twenty20 tournament known as the Big Bash League (BBL), which is based on franchises, has developed into a commercial success that has attracted investment and created economic prospects.

The Indian Premier League (IPL) is not only an enormous draw for cricket fans in India but also an important driver of the country's economy. In addition to fostering tourism and providing a boost for local companies, it results in huge financial gains and employment prospects.

The expansion of cricket infrastructure, which includes stadiums and training facilities, helps to contribute to the expansion of the economy. In addition, cricket's economic influence extends to tourism, since the sport's international events are known to draw large crowds of spectators who in turn help boost local economies.

5. **Women's Cricket and the Changing Dynamics of Gender**

Players and spectators do not need to be male to participate in cricket. Significant progress has been made toward achieving gender parity, and women's cricket has been at the forefront of this movement. The rise of female cricketers as sporting heroes and role models has led to an increase in the amount of support and participation that is given to female cricket players.

A new generation of female cricketers has emerged as a direct result of the achievements of teams such as the Indian Women's Cricket Team and the Australian Women's Cricket Team, also known as the Southern Stars. In addition to being a source of empowerment, women's cricket also serves as a mirror for the shifting gender dynamics that are occurring within the sport.

Women's cricket has made significant strides forward in a number of countries, including England and New Zealand, in terms of securing professional contracts and gaining respect. This move reflects a broader shift in society's attitude toward recognizing the contributions that women have made to sports.

The growing significance of gender equality and the larger impact of cricket on the progression of society are reflected in the development of women's cricket over the past few decades.

6. **Obstacles and Points of Controversy**

The sport of cricket is not without its share of difficulties and debates. Scandals involving match-fixing and corruption, as well as problems with governance, have dogged the sport. Concerns about ethics have been raised as a result of the impact of money and commercial interests, which threatens the game's overall integrity.

Disputes between cricket boards are only one example of how governance and administrative issues have frequently diverted attention away from the actual sport of cricket. In addition to being a substantial obstacle, the fight for inclusivity and diversity in cricket has been an uphill battle, and there are still continuous efforts being made to advance equity within the sport.

As a result of these obstacles, it is even more important for cricket to uphold high standards of transparency, accountability, and ethical behavior, since resolving these problems is essential to the development of the sport.

7. **The Contemporary Era and Its Accompanying Technological Developments**

The modern era of cricket has seen a tremendous amount of development in both the format of the game and the role that technology plays in cricket. The viewing experience has been improved thanks to technological developments such as Hawk-Eye for decision reviews and real-time analytics, which have made the experience more participatory and immersive for the audience.

The sport has been completely transformed as a result of the implementation of shorter formats such as One Day Internationals (ODIs) and Twenty20 (T20) cricket matches. These formats appeal to a variety of audiences by providing exciting action and entertainment at a breakneck pace.

The development of franchise-based Twenty20 competitions, such as the Indian Premier League (IPL) and the Big Bash League (BBL), has resulted in the gathering of players from all over the world and the interest of spectators from all over the world. Cricket has been turned into a year-round spectacle because to the establishment of many leagues, which has helped to broaden the sport's audience and broaden its appeal.

8. **International Conflicts and Diplomacy through the Game of Cricket**

Cricket has the extraordinary capacity to encourage cooperation on a global scale and can even be used as an instrument of diplomacy on occasion. The use of sports as a tool for conducting diplomacy and reducing tensions between India and Pakistan has been an important contributor to the success of recent conversations between the two countries. Cricket matches are frequently used as venues for intercultural dialogue and diplomatic initiatives.

The cricketing competition between India and Sri Lanka has also played a part in the diplomatic relationship between the two countries. For example, during India's tour of Sri Lanka in 2004, which followed the year's tragic tsunami, cricket matches became a symbol of togetherness and optimism for the people of Sri Lanka.

In a similar vein, cricket has the ability to strengthen international relations between states, with matches acting as occasions for diplomatic interaction and the construction of bridges between countries.

9. **The Impact of Climate Change on the Development of Cricket**

The impact of climate change is becoming an increasingly important obstacle in cricket. Changing weather patterns can have an impact on the scheduling of matches, which can cause tournaments to be disrupted and create playing conditions that present difficulties for players. A growing problem that needs to be addressed is the potential influence that climate change will have on the future of the sport.

10. **The Changing Experience of the Fans**

The advent of the internet age has completely revolutionized the cricket fan experience. Fans can participate with the sport by following matches in real time, accessing statistics and analysis, and participating in online communities thanks to social media and the internet.

The advent of the digital age has made cricket more approachable and participatory for spectators, enabling them to form connections with the sport on a worldwide scale.

Cricket is much more than just a sport; it is a passion with deep roots that has a significant impact on the development of nations. Its cultural significance, capacity to bring together people of different backgrounds, and political influence all underscore the role it plays in the formation of national identities. The economic impact of cricket helps nations develop, while the expansion of women's cricket reflects changing gender dynamics within the sport. Together, these two factors contribute to the growth of cricket. Even if it is plagued by difficulties and debates, the sport still welcomes advances in technology and acts as a medium for international communication. As cricket looks to the future, tackling the issue of climate change and improving the experience of fans will be important to the sport's ability to maintain its appeal on a worldwide scale. The ongoing impact that cricket has had on the development of nations is illustrative of the force and significance that the sport possesses on the international scene.

Chapter 1

The Birth of Cricket

Cricket is a sport that has its beginnings deeply ingrained in the history and culture of England. Through its development and subsequent global expansion, cricket has become a modern-day sport that is played and enjoyed by millions of people all over the world. This exhaustive investigation of the beginnings of cricket dives into the earliest forms of the game, its evolution into a pastime for members of the British upper class, and its subsequent expansion across continents and countries. The history of cricket, from its modest origins to its ascent as a global phenomenon, represents not only the development of a sport but also the societal changes and ideals that have affected its trajectory over the centuries. From its humble beginnings, cricket has risen to become a global phenomenon.

1. **Predecessors and Emergence in the Early Years (13th-16th Century)**

   It is possible to trace the origins of cricket all the way back to the medieval era in England, where a variety of games were played with a ball and a bat at the center of the action. These early iterations of cricket went by a variety of names and lacked the defined rules and regulations that have come to characterize the game as we know it today. The games were typically played in open areas, and players would use basic bats made of wood to strike a ball made of rags or another small, hard material.

   In the historical records of the 16th century, references to "crockett" and "criquet" started to occur, which is a clear indication that the game was becoming increasingly popular. These allusions suggest that cricket was already gaining popularity as a sport among the people of England, despite the fact that the specific rules and structures of the early game remain rather opaque.

2. **The Development into an Elegant Passtime in the Seventeenth Century**

   The beginning of the 17th century was an important turning point in the development of cricket, as this was the time when the game first started to take on a more structured format. The rise of cricket as a popular pastime for members of the upper class in British society resulted in the formation of clubs and the beginning of organized matches. The game's rules and practices were significantly influenced by members of the nobility and gentry of the historical period, who were also instrumental in creating the framework for the game's further evolution.

The earliest documented mention to a formal cricket match was made in the year 1646, which highlights the rising acceptance of cricket as a sport that can be played competitively. The establishment of early cricket clubs such as the Hambledon Club in the 1760s was an important step in the process of codifying the game's rules and regulations, and it was one of the first steps taken in this direction. In addition, the emergence of cricket as a significant leisure sport for the English upper class can be partially attributed to the contributions made by these clubs.

3. **The Marylebone Cricket Club and the Beginnings of Standardization in the 18th Century**

The Marylebone Cricket Club (MCC) was established as a central authority for the sport of cricket during the 18th century, which was also the same century that saw the formalization of cricket's regulations. The important part that the MCC played in establishing and enforcing the Laws of Cricket, which were initially published in 1788, contributed to the codification of the regulations that are still used to control the game today. These laws served as the basis for the contemporary rules of cricket, including those pertaining to the dimensions of the field, the dimensions of the equipment, and the directions for the gaming.

The MCC's influence was felt well beyond the confines of the local sphere, as the organization was instrumental in the staging of international cricket matches and the promotion of the growth of the sport on a worldwide scale. The rules and regulations established by the MCC played a significant role in standardizing the game of cricket and establishing the framework for the sport's eventual globalization in the centuries to come.

4. **Became Common Throughout the British Empire in the 19th Century**

During the 19th century, cricket saw a period of fast expansion as the game made its way across the British Empire, particularly in areas such as Australia, India, and the West Indies. This time is known as the Golden Age of Cricket. The British colonial officials, military personnel, and settlers had a crucial role in introducing cricket to these territories, which led to the sport fast gaining popularity among the native populations. Cricket was originally played with a bat and ball.

The spread of cricket to other parts of the world was aided by the formation of cricket clubs and the staging of matches in former British colonies. The first international cricket match was played between the United States and Canada in 1844. Subsequently, the format of Test cricket was developed, which further reinforced the game's appeal on a global scale and set the way for its ongoing legacy as a worldwide athletic phenomenon.

5. **The progression of the modern game into the twenty-first century and beyond**

The sport of cricket was forced to adapt to the shifting preferences of an international audience over the 20th century, which resulted in considerable changes to the format and structure of the game. The advent of One-Day Internationals (ODIs) in the 1970s and the following development of Twenty20 (T20) cricket in the 21st century brought about a sea change in both the way the game was played and how it was followed by fans around the world.

Cricket has been converted into a multi-billion dollar industry as a result of increased commercialization, the growth of international competitions such as the Cricket World Cup, and the establishment of franchise-based leagues such as the Indian Premier League (IPL) and the Big Bash League (BBL). These improvements not only helped to broaden the appeal of cricket and boost its popularity, but they also helped to usher in a brand-new era of professionalism and commercialization inside the cricketing world.

6. **The Impact of Cricket on a Global Scale and Its Significance to Culture**

The inception of cricket, from its humble beginnings as a rural pastime to its current status as a global sporting spectacle, has had a significant influence on the cultural and social fabric of nations all over the world. Cricket's humble beginnings as a rural pastime can be contrasted with its current status as a global athletic spectacle. Cricket is now much more than just a game; it is a mirror of cultural ideals, a source of national pride, and a unifying force for communities that are very different from one another.

Cricket's popularity in India has reached heights that have never been seen before, and the game is now seen as a unifying force for the entire country as well as a source of intense passion. The advent of renowned cricket players like Sachin Tendulkar and the founding of the Indian Premier League have solidified cricket's place as a cultural phenomenon inside the nation of India. [Cricket] is played all year long in the Indian Premier League.

Cricket has been a unifying force in the West Indies, which is an area comprised of several different nations with their own distinct traditions. Not only have the accomplishments of cricketing greats such as Sir Vivian Richards and Brian Lara contributed to the sport's rise to popularity, but they have also given the people of the Caribbean a strong feeling of national pride and identity.

In a similar manner, cricket has become an essential component of national identity in both England and Australia. Long-standing competitions, such as the Ashes, serve as cultural touchstones that conjure a feeling of tradition and lineage.

The fact that cricket was originally played in India is evidence of the sport's long history, which has persisted through many eras, locations, and cultural norms. Cricket is now a worldwide phenomenon that brings people together and plays a role in the formation of national identities. Its humble beginnings may be traced back to the countryside of England, but it has since gained enormous popularity across continents.

The foundation for the present version of cricket was built by the game's development from an unstructured hobby into a competitive sport, as well as by the Marylebone Cricket Club's efforts to standardize the sport after its inception. The rise of cricket to unprecedented heights can be attributed to the globalization of the sport, which was fueled by the expansion of the British Empire and the beginning of international competitions.

The advent of the modern age of cricket, which is defined by shorter forms and commercialization, has resulted in the sport's expansion into a global market and the creation of an enterprise worth multiple billions of dollars. Countries that are passionate about cricket, such as India, the West Indies, Australia, and England, all display clear signs of the game's influence on their culture, society, and sense of national pride.

As the 21st century progresses, cricket is serving as a living example of the enduring power of sports to unite communities, instill a sense of national pride, and mirror the norms and ideals of a variety of countries. This is a tribute to the sport's role as a unifying force. The origins of cricket, as well as the sport's continued development, provide a captivating account of how a straightforward game played with a bat and ball can develop into a phenomenon that transcends national lines and persists for hundreds of years.

1.1 The origins of cricket in England

Since the dawn of time, England has been virtually inseparable from the sport of cricket, which boasts a long and illustrious pedigree. In England, cricket can be traced back to the medieval period, when it was a straightforward yet popular activity that was played in open fields and meadows. During this time, the game was played on open fields and meadows. This essay investigates the early history of cricket in England, tracing its progression from a rural pastime to a competitive sport and analyzing the significant part it played in the development of the sporting culture of the country.

1. **The Beginnings of Medieval Times: A Countryside Passtime (13th-16th Century)**

   The use of bats and balls in a variety of sports that were popular in England during the middle ages can be traced back to the origins of cricket. These basic games consisted of hitting a ball with a bat or club, and they were typically played in open areas, such as village greens, with a limited amount of standardization or regulations. Even though these early forms of cricket were not the same as the game as it is played today, they were crucial in laying the groundwork for the development of the sport.

Old English names like "cric" or "cryce" and the French word "criquet," all of which allude to sports combining a ball and a curved club, have been suggested as possible origins for the word "cricket." However, the exact origin of the word "cricket" remains unknown. These early games were popular past times that were enjoyed by people of all ages and backgrounds; nevertheless, they lacked the established rules and organized competition that would later come to define cricket in later centuries.

2. **The Beginnings of Formalization and Record Keeping (17th Century)**

    The sport of cricket took its initial tentative moves toward becoming more organized throughout the 17th century. The game started to develop popularity and structure at the same time as documented references to cricket started to appear in historical records. The English populace had already begun to take an interest in the game, which was already well on its way to transforming from an unorganized country pleasure into a competitive sport.

    Written sources from the 17th century contain some of the first known references to the sport of cricket. A little child was injured in Sussex in the year 1598 when he was hit in the head by a cricket ball, which is evidence that the sport was popular at the time. Additionally, around the year 1611, an English attorney named John Derrick mentioned the game in his will. Specifically, he mentioned "crockett" as an activity that he had enjoyed doing as a child.

3. **The Impact of the British Aristocracy (During the 17th to 18th Centuries)**

    The interests of the British upper class were strongly tied to the development of cricket into an official sport and pastime in the United Kingdom. As a result of the contributions by members of the nobility and gentry, the rules and traditions of the game were effectively transformed from those of a popular leisure into those of a sport associated with the upper class.

    The first cricket clubs, which were initially more like social meetings than organized sporting groups, were founded in the 17th century. These clubs, such as the Hambledon Club in Hampshire, played a significant part in the formulation and standardization of the game's rules, which was an important step in the game's history. They made important contributions to the evolution of cricket into a sport that is more structured and competitive.

    The participation of members of the British upper class not only influenced the development of the sport but also laid the groundwork for the continuation of cricket's rise in popularity as a recreational pastime among the country's upper classes.

4. **The Marylebone Cricket Club in the 18th century was instrumental in the formalization of the game's rules**

    The Marylebone Cricket Club (MCC) was established as a central authority for the sport of cricket during the 18th century, which was an important phase in the formalization of cricket's regulations. In the process of formulating the rules that are still in effect for the game today, the MCC was an essential contributor. The Marylebone Cricket Club (MCC) was the organization that first issued the "Laws of Cricket" in 1788. These regulations were intended to serve as a foundation for the growth of the sport. These laws covered important facets of the game, such as the dimensions of the playing field, the types of equipment that might be used, and the rules governing how to play the game. The current game of cricket adheres to the majority of these restrictions to this day.

The MCC's effect was not confined to the confines of the home sphere. The club was instrumental in the coordination of cricket competitions on a global scale and in the growth of the sport overall, playing a pivotal role in both of these endeavors. The efforts made by the MCC to codify the rules provided the groundwork for the global development of cricket, and the game's laws continue to serve as an essential component of the present version of the sport.

5. **The Effects of Colonial Exploration and Development (19th Century)**

The 19th century was characterized by the spread of cricket outside the borders of England. During this time period, British colonial administrators, military troops, and settlers were responsible for introducing the sport to numerous countries around the British Empire. In these colonial regions, the indigenous people enthusiastically took up cricket, which led to the sport's meteoric rise in popularity.

For example, Australia was one of the earliest countries outside of England to embrace the sport of cricket. The sport became popular among the indigenous people of Australia as well as the European settlers, and it continued to gain popularity throughout the 19th century.

During this time period, the Indian subcontinent also acquired a significant fondness for the sport of cricket. The British Raj was a significant contributor to the development of cricket in the region, which led to an increase in the sport's popularity among the upper classes in India.

During the middle of the 19th century, the first cricket matches in India were played in Bombay, which is now known as Mumbai. Soon after, cricket clubs started cropping up all over the subcontinent.

These former colonial areas proved to be fruitful ground for the spread of cricket across the world. A crucial step forward for cricket's development on the global stage was taken in 1844 when the United States and Canada competed in the first international cricket match. This event served as a catalyst for the sport's expansion into new territories across the world.

It is possible to trace the history of cricket in England all the way back to the middle ages, when it was a basic country game that was played in open fields with rudimentary equipment and few if any rules. Cricket has transformed over the course of several centuries from a casual pastime into a competitive sport, in part because members of the British upper class have been actively participating in the game. In the 17th and 18th centuries, cricket clubs and the formalization of the game's rules emerged, with the Marylebone Cricket Club (MCC) playing a pivotal part in the process of defining the game's regulations.

The spread of cricket across the British Empire in the 19th century was a significant factor in the development of cricket into a phenomenon that is observed all over the world. In places like Australia and the Indian subcontinent, the development of cricket was made possible in large part by the influence of colonial officials and settlers, who, together with the enthusiasm of the native people, cleared the way for the sport's expansion.

Not only does the origin of cricket in England signify the development of a sport, but it also exemplifies the larger historical, cultural, and societal shifts that have contributed to the sport's progression. The extraordinary journey that cricket took from its meager origins to its current position as a treasured leisure for millions of people all over the world is reflected in its enduring legacy as a sport with global relevance.

1.2 Early rules and development of the game

The sport of cricket, which has deep historical origins, has developed over the course of centuries, and the early regulations and evolution of the game have played an important role in contributing to the game as we know it today. Cricket went from being a rural pastime to a standardized sport over the course of its history, and this transition can be traced back to the game's rules and regulations, which underwent considerable adjustments over time. This essay examines the growth of cricket from its more primitive beginnings to the introduction of fundamental regulations that continue to regulate the game. The study goes into the early rules and development of cricket and explores the evolution of the sport.

1. **Predecessors from an Early Stage and Unstructured Play**
   The history of cricket may be traced back to medieval England, a time period in which a variety of bat-and-ball sports were played for recreation in England. In these earlier incarnations of the game, there were no set rules, and matches were frequently played in a casual and impromptu manner. Players used basic equipment like wooden bats to hit a ball made of rags or a small, hard object. This ball was used as the target for the game.

   However, despite the fact that people of all ages and walks of life participated in these early games, they were nothing like the organized and regulated sport that we know and love today. Early iterations of the game of cricket were open to a number of different interpretations of the rules, which resulted in significant regional differences in the manner in which the game was played.

2. **The First Written Records and the Establishment of Early Rules (around the 17th Century)**

The 17th century was a pivotal time in the evolution of cricket, which represented a critical turning point. The beginning of written records during this time period offers extremely helpful insights into the early structure of the game as well as its governing regulations. Certain fundamental features started to materialize, despite the fact that the rules were not defined and there was still a great deal of variety in the way cricket was played.

The "Articles of Agreement" of the Bramley and Hambledon Cricket Clubs from 1709 is a remarkable example from this time period. These "Articles of Agreement" established the rules and regulations for matches that were played between the two clubs. These early rules covered a variety of characteristics of the game, like as the dimensions of the pitch and wickets, as well as how disagreements were to be resolved. This document offers an insight into the efforts being made to standardize the rules of cricket and create recommendations for how the game should be played.

3. **The Founding of the Marylebone Cricket Club (MCC) and the Development of the Rules of Cricket in the 18th Century**

   Important steps toward the formalization of cricket's regulations and the founding of the Marylebone Cricket Club (MCC) as the primary governing body for the sport were both accomplished during the 18th century. The contribution of the MCC to the development of the Laws of Cricket was critical to the establishment of a consistent basis for the play of the game.

   In the year 1788, the MCC issued the Laws of Cricket, a document that would go on to serve as the basis for the regulations governing cricket.

   These regulations covered important aspects of the game, like the dimensions of the pitch, the building of the wicket, bowling techniques, and the guidelines for the gameplay. A good number of these restrictions were crucial in laying the foundation for the current cricket rules.

   The MCC's effect was felt well beyond the borders of England because of the significant part it played in the organization of international cricket matches and the promotion of the growth of the sport on a worldwide scale. The devotion of the MCC to standardizing the rules of cricket helped pave the way for the game's development to other countries and contributed to the game's ongoing popularity.

4. **Early Equipment and Conditions of the Playing Field**

   In the early days of cricket, the equipment used and the playing conditions on the pitch were

   significantly different from what is expected today. The majority of bats were handcrafted from willow and had a very straight profile. The balls were made of leather and did not have the same degree of uniformity in terms of shape and size as cricket balls used today. The actual pitch was

   frequently uneven and required regular care to be kept in good condition.

Conditions on the playing field were taken into consideration extensively when drafting the rules for the game. As competitions became more organized, there was an increased emphasis placed on maintaining a uniform playing surface. In order to create an equal playing field, the dimensions of the pitches (both in length and width) were standardized, and regulations concerning the preparation and maintenance of the pitches were written down.

5. **Bowling Methods, Including Overhead and Underarm Bowling**
Since the beginning of the game of cricket, there has been a substantial evolution in the bowling techniques used. The underarm delivery method was the most common one employed by bowlers in the 18th century. This method involved delivering the ball with the arm swinging below the waist. Even though it was successful, this approach had restrictions when it came to pace and variety.

Overarm bowling was one of the most major rule changes in the history of cricket. This rule permitted bowlers to deliver the ball with their arm extended above their shoulder, which was one of the most significant rule changes in cricket's history. This development, which took place in the middle of the 19th century, completely altered the nature of the sport by making it possible for bowlers to generate a greater amount of pace and spin.

The adoption of overarm bowling marked a significant departure from the traditional style of play in cricket, and it had a significant influence on the evolution of the game as well as its strategic approach. This modification to the way bowling was performed helped to contribute to the wide variety of bowling styles observed in current cricket.

6. **Earlier Scoring and the Scoring Systems Used**
Runs were initially tallied by physically marking lines or holes on the ground, which resulted in a crude method of scoring in the early days of cricket. As the competition got more organized, there was an increased emphasis placed on the creation of standardized scoring systems. Formalized techniques of scoring were developed around the same time as the idea of runs being scored and wickets being taken started to take shape.

Early methods of keeping score consisted of making basic notations and tally marks, which were typically written down on a chalkboard or sheet of paper. The introduction of more complex scoring procedures, such as the use of scorebooks and scorecards, led to improvements in both the accuracy and efficiency of recording the results of matches and the statistics of individual players.

7. **The Development of Various Playing Formats**

The earliest forms of cricket were not played according to the standardized formats that are used in current cricket. The time allotted for each match was subject to change but typically ranged from several days to even weeks. The idea of innings, as well as the division between the side that bats and the side that fields, gradually emerged throughout time.

The idea of "innings" was first introduced in the 19th century, and during that time period, each team was given the opportunity to bat and bowl in turn. This evolution resulted in the creation of longer forms of the game, such as Test cricket, in which matches may continue for several days.

The conventional, multi-day structure of cricket was significantly altered when shorter forms such as one-day internationals (ODIs) and twenty20 (T20) matches were introduced. This marked a substantial departure from the standard format. These changes suited to the shifting preferences of the audience by providing versions of the game that were faster-paced and easier to understand.

The transformation of cricket from a casual hobby into a planned and organized game is a fascinating topic to explore, and its early rules and development offer some fascinating insight into this transition.

The creation of rules and regulations that regulated how the game was played was a defining moment in cricket's evolution from its more rudimentary beginnings to its modern, standardized format. This event marked the beginning of cricket's modern era.

It is impossible to overstate the importance of the Marylebone Cricket Club's (MCC) role in the development of cricket as a sport and the laws that govern it. Cricket was shaped into the worldwide phenomenon that it is today in large part by the introduction of overarm bowling, the development of scoring systems, and the growth of playing formats.

The narrative of how cricket's early laws and evolution came to be highlights the adaptability of the sport as well as its everlasting attraction. It also shows the constant endeavor to find a balance between preserving tradition and embracing innovation, which is a trademark of the game's rich history. This work has been going on for quite some time. The potential of cricket to evolve and remain relevant over the course of several centuries is demonstrated by the sport's progression from its rural beginnings to its current standing as a game played all over the world.

1.3 The spread of cricket to other nations

Cricket is a sport that was first played in England but has since spread across countries and cultures, winning the hearts of millions of people all over the world. The path of the sport's spread to other countries is a trip of cultural interchange, the passion of sporting competition, and the fraternity of the world. From its beginnings in British colonial territories to its current-day popularity on a global scale, cricket has been able to transcend national borders, leaving an indelible impression on the social, cultural, and sporting landscapes of a wide variety of countries. This in-depth investigation digs into the important milestones and transformative moments that have molded the expansion of cricket to other countries, revealing its impact on communities, national identities, and the greater fabric of international sportsmanship along the way.

1. **The Establishment of New Colonies and the Growing Power of the British Empire**

The influence of the British Empire, which introduced the sport to many locations across the world during the time period known as the colonial era, can be credited with the propagation of cricket in areas of the world other than England. Cricket was brought to the colonies by British colonial officials, military troops, and settlers, all of whom played an essential part in the process. Once cricket was introduced, its popularity among the native people of each colony grew rapidly.

In Australia, a country that was once a colony of the United Kingdom, cricket became the country's most popular sport.

The sport was first played in what is now known as India in the 18th century, which is widely regarded as the beginning of the country's illustrious cricketing legacy. India is known for producing some of the sport's most renowned players and staging some of the most famous contests.

In a similar vein, the countries of the Indian subcontinent, which include India, Pakistan, and Sri Lanka, developed into key hubs for the sport of cricket as a direct result of the introduction of the sport by British colonialists. In a short amount of time, cricket was able to break through societal, cultural, and language obstacles and establish itself as an indispensable component of the region's shared sense of identity.

During the time of colonial rule, cricket became deeply ingrained in the culture of the West Indies, which is comprised of several different Caribbean nations. The sport evolved into a unifying force for the region, helping to cultivate a feeling of communal pride and identity that extended beyond the boundaries of the individual island states.

2. **The Organization of Matches and Competitions on an International Scale**

The 19th century was a pivotal time in the development of cricket as a sport around the world since it was the century in which the first official international cricket matches were played. Cricket's expansion onto the world scene was catalyzed by the first ever international match, which took place in 1844 and included a contest between the United States of America and Canada.

The following creation of Test cricket, a format in which matches are played over the course of many days, contributed significantly to the sport's growing popularity on an international scale. Since its inception in 1882, the Ashes series, which is played between England and Australia, has been a shining example of the spirit of transcontinental competitiveness and friendship. It has also been responsible for the development of a sense of friendly rivalry that has persisted for more than a century.

The development of other prominent competitions, such as the Cricket World Cup, brought together nations from different continents in a celebration of athletic brilliance and international sportsmanship. This served to draw attention to the worldwide relevance of the sport.

3. **The Influence of Cricket on Other Continents and Cultures (Third Section)**
The sport of cricket has expanded beyond its colonial roots, and as a result, it has been able to transcend geographical boundaries and resonate with a wide variety of people and cultures across continents.

The sport's popularity in countries like South Africa, New Zealand, and Zimbabwe is evidence that it has the power to form connections and encourage a sense of shared passion and pride.

Cricket's role as a unifying factor during the fight against apartheid is only one example of how South Africa's complex past is reflected in the country's illustrious cricketing history. The inclusion of players from a wide range of backgrounds on South Africa's national cricket team, which competes under the name "Proteas," exemplifies the nation's dedication to fostering an inclusive and varied sporting environment.

The passion that the people of New Zealand have for cricket has strong cultural origins, and the sport has become deeply ingrained in the nation's social fabric. The accomplishments of the New Zealand cricket team have instilled a sense of national pride and solidarity, showcasing the power of sport to bring people together in times of triumph and friendship.

The journey that Zimbabwe has taken in cricket has been marked by both victories and setbacks, which is reflective of the nation's resiliency and tenacity. In spite of the socio-political challenges that have been presented, the sport has offered Zimbabweans a stage upon which they can exhibit their skills and pursue their interests, exemplifying the qualities of tenacity and national pride.

4. **The Rise of Cricketing Superpowers and the International Arena of Competition**
The 20th and 21st centuries have seen the growth of cricketing powerhouses outside of the traditional strongholds of England and Australia. These new powerhouses include India, Pakistan, and South Africa. As a result of their fervent fan bases and great players, countries like India, Pakistan, and Sri Lanka have emerged as strong competitors on the international scene. This is due to the fact that these nations have significantly contributed to the sport's ability to compete successfully on a global scale.

The steadfast devotion of the Indian people to the game of cricket has been essential to the country's meteoric rise to the top of the cricketing world rankings. Since its inception in 2008, the Indian Premier League (IPL) has been a game-changer in the world of cricket. It has been successful in luring the best players from across the world and in highlighting India's economic and sports strength on a worldwide scale.

Cricket in Pakistan has a long and illustrious history, which, along with the tenacity of its players, has left a lasting legacy.

In spite of the obstacles that it has had to overcome, the country has been able to create cricket players of a world-class level and has shown a remarkable capacity to compete at the top levels of the sport. This is an example of the spirit of perseverance and dedication.

Cricket's dominance in Sri Lanka has been a wellspring of national pride, with the country's victory in the Cricket World Cup in 1996 serving as a watershed point in its long and illustrious athletic tradition. The accomplishments of Sri Lankan cricketers have served as a source of motivation for younger generations and have reaffirmed the nation's dedication to superior performance and sportsmanship.

5. **The growth of franchise-based leagues in conjunction with globalization**

The 21st century has seen the globalization of cricket, with the establishment of franchise-based leagues that have turned the sport into a commercial and entertainment spectacle. This globalization has occurred with the globalization of entertainment. Cricket has undergone a landscape revolution thanks to the advent of tournaments like as the Indian Premier League (IPL), the Big Bash League (BBL), and the Caribbean Premier League (CPL). These competitions have attracted the best players from all over the world and captivated an audience on a global scale.

The success of these leagues has not only raised the profiles of the countries that are taking part in the competitions, but it has also helped to the development of cricket as a lucrative sector, which has resulted in significant money and fostered economic growth in the countries that are hosting the competitions.

6. **The Influence of Cricket on Societal Transformation and Diplomacy**

Cricket has often been used as a catalyst for social change and diplomacy. It has played a crucial part in the development of international relations and in the promotion of cultural exchanges between nations. The historic cricket series between India and Pakistan has been a classic example of how sport can overcome political divisions, encourage people-to-people interactions, and build a spirit of friendliness and collaboration. The series was played between India and Pakistan in the month of October.

In a similar vein, cricket has been essential in fostering unity and reconciliation in regions that have historically been plagued by a variety of socio-political issues. Because of its potential to unite people from all over the world and break down barriers, sport has emerged as a potent force in the ongoing effort to build world peace, tolerance, and respect for one another on a worldwide scale.

7. **The Development of Women's Sports and Cricket for Females**

It is illustrative of the larger movement toward gender equality and inclusiveness in sports that the expansion of women's cricket has been a game-changing development in the journey of the sport around the world. Women's cricket is gaining popularity as a result of the proliferation of international contests and leagues that provide female players the chance to display their skills and demonstrate their dedication to the sport.

A new generation of female athletes has been inspired by the triumphs of women's cricket teams in nations such as Australia, England, and India. This highlights the potential for growth and recognition within the women's sporting arena.

The story of cricket's growth to other countries is one of cross-cultural interaction, the fervor of competitive sports, and the brotherhood of people all across the world. In spite of its colonial beginnings and current prominence as a global phenomenon, cricket has managed to transcend geographical boundaries and find a place in a wide variety of communities and cultural contexts all over the world.

The sport's growth beyond its traditional strongholds has demonstrated its ability to bring people from different countries together, to encourage social transformation, and to facilitate international cooperation. The development of cricketing power-houses, the appearance of leagues based on franchises, and the expansion of women's cricket have all helped to add to the sport's enduring appeal and significant impact on the competitive landscape of sports around the world.

It is a credit to cricket's ability to unite people, celebrate diversity, and inspire brilliance on the international stage that the sport was able to make its way from the English countryside all the way into the hearts of millions of people across several continents. The story of how cricket became popular in other countries is about more than just a sport; it is also a tale of ideals that people around the world hold in common, the power of emotion, and the enduring spirit of sportsmanship.

Chapter 2

Cricket and National Identity

Cricket, which is frequently referred to as something other than merely a sport, has a significant and complicated connection to the national identities of the countries in which it is played. This essay of 3000 words explores into the complex relationships that exist between cricket and national identity. Specifically, it examines how the sport has become a reflection of a nation's culture, history, and core beliefs for countries all over the world. Cricket serves as a lens through which we can understand the complex interplay of tradition, politics, and societal aspirations that define a nation's identity. Its origins can be traced back to England, and the game has since taken on a variety of forms in countries such as India, Australia, the West Indies, and Pakistan, among other places.

1. **The Opening Statements**
   The Unbreakable Bond Between Cricket and a Country's Sense of Itself
   The sport of cricket, which is played with a willow bat and a leather ball, is more than just a leisure activity. It is the embodiment of the values, traditions, and collective identity of the countries in which it is played with great passion. According to a well-known quote attributed to W.G. Grace, "Cricket is the greatest thing that God ever created." In this article of 3000 words, we investigate the complex connection that exists between cricket and national identity, beginning with the game's beginnings in England and moving on to its modern manifestations in countries such as India, Australia, the West Indies, Pakistan, and many more. The narrative of cricket as a mirror of culture, history, and aspirations enables us to get a glimpse of the complex interaction of tradition, politics, and societal values that create a nation's identity. This is made possible by the fact that cricket originated in India.

2. **Cricket's Origins in the United Kingdom**
   Cricket was originally a country sport that was played in open fields in England throughout the middle ages. Its roots may be traced back to this time period. The

game originated from a variety of other pastimes involving bats and balls, and it quickly gained popularity among players from many walks of life. In its earliest iterations, cricket did not have a set of defined rules and regulations, which reflected the more casual nature of the game throughout its formative years.

3. **The Evolving Landscape of Cricket in England**

   Cricket went through a period of transition during the 17th and 18th century, during which it went from being a casual pastime to a formalized and organized sport. As members of the British aristocracy began to play the game, it went from being a popular pastime to being regarded as an elite sport. As a result of their influence, the game's rules and traditions are largely what they are today.

   The establishment of cricket clubs such as the Hambledon Club and the Marylebone Cricket Club (MCC), which published the Laws of Cricket in 1788, were important steps in the process of standardizing the game. These events represented the evolution of cricket from an unstructured game to a sport with established rules and guidelines for play.

4. **The Role of Cricket as a Symbol of Being English**

   Cricket eventually grew entwined with the English identity, becoming a reflection of the nation's norms, beliefs, and customs. The game was seen to be a mirror of the English spirit because of its emphasis on qualities such as sportsmanship, fair play, and obedience to the rules. Beyond the boundaries of the playing field, cricket's influence has permeated many aspects of English culture and society.

5. **The Spread of Colonialism and the Internationalization of Cricket**

   The British Empire was instrumental in bringing cricket to other regions of the world and spreading its popularity. The game was brought to a number of British colonies by administrators, military personnel, and settlers from the mother country. These colonies included Australia, the Indian subcontinent, and the West Indies.

6. **Australia: Cricket and the Proudness of the Nation**

   Cricket rose to prominence in Australia quite fast, becoming the country's most cherished national sport. The history of cricket in this country is long and illustrious, involving players who went on to become legends and incidents that will live in infamy. The Ashes series played against England has evolved into a metaphor for the friendly competition that exists across oceans.

7. **The Indian Subcontinent: The Phenomenon of Cricket as a Cultural Icon**

   Cricket was enthusiastically taken up by the nations that make up the Indian subcontinent, including India, Pakistan, and Sri Lanka, amongst others. The game was able to overcome linguistic, cultural, and religious boundaries, and it eventually became an essential component of the region's overall sense of identity. The Indian Premier League (IPL) brought global attention to India's growing economic and sporting might, and it ushered in a new era for the sport of cricket.

8. **The West Indies: Cricket's Role as a Unifying Force in the Region**
Cricket served as a unifying force for the West Indies, which is comprised of several different Caribbean nations. A sense of community pride and identity that transcended particular island nations was established via the participation in the sport. The prominence of the sport in that region was increased by legendary players such as Sir Vivian Richards and Brian Lara.

9. **Pakistan: Cricket and the Art of Keeping Going**
Pakistan has a history of producing cricket players of world-class caliber and has shown an amazing capacity to compete at the top levels despite the difficulties it has faced. Cricket has acted as a source of national pride and solidarity, reflecting the resiliency and tenacity of the nation it has brought together.

10. **South Africa: Cricket and the Fight Against Apartheid in South Africa**
The complicated history of South Africa is inextricably linked with its rich cricketing heritage. The sport was extremely important in the fight against apartheid, and the inclusive and diverse make-up of South Africa's national cricket team, known as the Proteas, exemplifies the nation's dedication to diversity and inclusivity in all aspects of life.

11. **Cricket and the Formation of New Zealand's National Identity**
Cricket is ingrained in the culture of New Zealand and has a significant impact on the social makeup of the country. A sense of national pride and solidarity has been generated as a result of the sport, demonstrating the power that sports have to bring people together.

12. **Women's Cricket: A Power That's Only Going to Grow**
The advancement of women's cricket as a sport has been a game-changing breakthrough that reflects a broader shift toward gender equality in the sporting world. Opportunities for female players to display their talent and dedication to the sport are made available by participation in international leagues and events.

13. **The Importance of Cricket to the Process of Social Transformation and Diplomacy**
Cricket has frequently been a driving force behind social movements and diplomatic initiatives. The historic cricket series between India and Pakistan has helped to transcend political barriers and increase people-to-people interactions, which has fostered goodwill and collaboration between the two countries. The sport has also been essential in fostering solidarity and reconciliation in regions that have historically been plagued by socio-political tensions.

14. **The Influence of Cricket on the Advancement of the Economy**
The game of cricket has evolved into a multi-billion dollar industry that contributes significantly to the economic growth of the countries that hold international tournaments. Cricket has evolved into a commercial and entertainment

extravaganza thanks to the success of tournaments such as the Indian Premier League (IPL).

15. **The Spread of Cricket Around the World**

The twenty-first century has been witness to the globalization of cricket, with the introduction of franchise-based leagues that have drawn top international talent and enthralled an audience all around the world. Cricket's landscape has been revolutionized thanks to competitions like the Indian Premier League (IPL) and the Big Bash League, which have highlighted the sport's commercial potential and worldwide reach.

Cricket and a nation's sense of identity are inextricably linked, with the sport acting as a kind of cultural barometer, historical record keeper, and symbol of societal ideals for countries all over the world. Cricket is a sport that embodies the subtle interaction of tradition, politics, and societal goals that form a nation's identity. Its origins can be traced back to England, and it is now played in a variety of countries throughout the world.

The history of cricket encompasses much more than just the use of a bat and ball; rather, it is a tale of people, communities, and countries coming together to celebrate their individual identities and the things that they are passionate about in common. The tremendous influence that cricket has on nations and regions is highlighted by the sport's contributions to social progress, diplomatic efforts, and economic growth.

As the game of cricket continues to develop in the 21st century, it serves as a demonstration of the enduring ability of sport to bring people together, honor differences, and motivate individuals to perform to the best of their abilities on the global stage. The inseparable bond that exists between cricket and a nation's sense of self-identity is a testament to the fact that cricket is more than just a sport; it is a manifestation of a people's sense of shared history, culture, and heritage.

2.1 Cricket's role in shaping national identity

Cricket, which is more than just a sport, has been an essential component in the formation of the national identities of a number of countries located all over the world. From its humble origins on the English village greens to its current status as a global phenomenon, cricket has woven itself into the fabric of society, reflecting the values, aspirations, and cultural nuances of the nations where it is passionately embraced. From its beginnings on the English village greens to its current status as a global phenomena, cricket has evolved from its English village green roots to become a global phenomenon. This in-depth investigation delves into the multifaceted role that cricket plays in the formation of national identities. It examines how the sport has served as a unifying force, a source of pride, and a platform for social change, diplomacy, and economic development in a variety of countries, including India, Australia, the West Indies, Pakistan, England, and other places. With the help of cricket, we are able to disentangle the intricate web of stories that have shaped the collective psyche and sense of belonging in these countries over the course of their history.

1. **The Opening Statements**
   The Contribution of Cricket to the Formation of National Identity: Cricket as a Uniting Force Across Borders and Cultures
   Cricket transcends its role as a sport and acts as a potent icon of national identity for countries all over the world as a result of its historical tradition and widespread appeal. Cricket has both reflected and shaped the values, aspirations, and collective consciousness of nations that have embraced it with passion and zeal from its humble beginnings in the English countryside to its metamorphosis into a worldwide cultural phenomena. Its humble beginnings were in rural England, and it has since transformed into a worldwide cultural phenomenon. In this exploration of 2,000 words, we delve into the multifaceted role that cricket plays in the formation of national identity. We highlight the significance of cricket as a unifying force, a source of pride, and a catalyst for social change, diplomacy, and economic development in a variety of countries, including India, Australia, the West Indies, Pakistan, England, and even further afield. Through the prism of cricket, we are able to untangle the intricate web of stories that have played a role in the development of a shared sense of belonging as well as the cultural legacy of these countries.

2. **The Power of Cricket to Bring People Together: The Example of India**
   Cricket is more than simply a sport in India; it is a unifying force that transcends the country's diverse cultural, linguistic, and socio-economic environment. In India, cricket is a sport that has been played since ancient times. The Indian Premier League (IPL), with its star-studded teams and frenetic fan base, is an example of the successful combination of cricket and entertainment that speaks to millions of people all over the country. People from all walks of life are able to communicate with one another through the medium of cricket, which contributes to the development of a common feeling of pride and national togetherness.

3. **The Role of Cricket in the Formation of Australian Identity: The Pride of a Sporting Nation**
   The passion of the Australian people for sports and the outdoors is reflected in the country's deep-seated attachment to cricket, which plays a significant role in the national psyche. The long-standing competition with England, known as the Ashes series, has evolved into a representation of national pride and a healthy dose of healthy competition. Beyond the confines of the playing field, cricket has played an important part in the formation of Australia's national character since it serves as a reflection of the country's commitment to endurance, resiliency, and fair play.

4. **Cricket in the West Indies: A Unifying Force Through the Sport**

   Cricket has become a unifying force and a representation of the West Indies' collective identity. The West Indies is comprised of numerous Caribbean nations. It is a testament to the power of sport to bridge geopolitical differences and promote a common sense of regional pride that this region has produced some of the best cricket players in the world despite the constraints posed by country boundaries and various cultural origins.

5. **Pakistan: The Role of Cricket in Strengthening the National Spirit**

   Because of Pakistan's deep love for the sport of cricket, the country has been able to pull through difficult times and feel a sense of pride as a result. Despite the fact that the country faces a number of socio-political issues, it has shown a remarkable ability to compete at the top levels of the game and has produced players who have gone down in history. Cricket has been a force for unification, bringing together individuals of varied backgrounds and helping to build a feeling of collective national identity.

6. **Cricket in England, a Game Steeped in History and an Example of True Sportsmanship**

   Cricket is a sport that honors its history and upholds the principles of sportsmanship and fair play in the country where it was first played. Cricket is a symbol of national pride and identity in England, and the sport's long and illustrious history in that country is a reflection of the country's deeply ingrained cultural legacy. The Marylebone Cricket Club (MCC), in its role as the custodian of the Laws of Cricket, promotes the spirit of the game as well as its traditional values, placing an emphasis on the significance of honesty and respect within the culture of cricket.

7. **The Role of Cricket in South Africa's Struggle for Inclusivity**

   Cricket has been an important part of South Africa's path toward unity and reconciliation, playing a crucial role in both the promotion of inclusiveness and diversity and in reflecting on that journey.

   South Africa's dedication to overcome historical differences and embracing a collective identity that celebrates diversity and equality is symbolized by the country's national cricket team, which is known as the Proteas. The team is made up of players from a variety of backgrounds.

8. **The sport of cricket as a vehicle for fostering social change and diplomatic relations**

   Cricket has often been used as a platform for social change and diplomacy, making it easier for people from different cultures to interact with one another and building goodwill across countries. The historic cricket series between India and Pakistan has served as a conduit for the promotion of people-to-people connections and the enhancement of bilateral relations. It has also helped to transcend political tensions while simultaneously fostering a culture of camaraderie and understanding.

9. **The Financial Effects of Cricket: How It Drives Development and Opportunity**

   The huge economic impact of cricket has spurred development and opportunity in a number of different nations, including the creation of employment possibilities, the promotion of tourism, and the promotion of infrastructural development. The cricketing landscape has been significantly altered as a result of competitions such as the Indian Premier League (IPL) and the Big Bash League (BBL). These competitions generate significant income and contribute to the economic prosperity of the nations that host them.

10. **Women's Cricket: Defining Identity and Offering a Platform for Empowerment**

Traditional narratives have been rewritten, and female athletes now have a stronger voice in the sporting arena as a direct result of the expansion of women's cricket. Women's cricket has evolved as a potent weapon for promoting gender equality and inclusivity. It gives female players opportunities to demonstrate their talent and passion, and it inspires a new generation of athletes to redefine the bounds of identity and achievement. These are all important goals for the sport.

The significance of cricket in the formation of national identities extends far beyond its role as a competitive sport; rather, it encapsulates the shared ideals, aspirations, and cultural traditions of countries all over the world. The influence of cricket may be felt well beyond the confines of the playing field, as the sport has been shown to do everything from promote national cohesion and resiliency to act as a stage for social reform, diplomatic efforts, and economic growth. The ongoing legacy of the sport as a force that brings people together and a symbol of pride exemplifies the deep influence that the sport has on the collective consciousness and sense of belonging in a variety of nations. As the 21st century progresses, cricket is serving as a living example of the power that sports have always had to mold and define a nation's identity while also bringing communities together and honoring the myriad ways in which people have lived their lives.

2.2 Iconic cricketing moments that united nations

Moments of transcendent significance have occurred in the game of cricket throughout its history, and their impact has been felt well beyond the boundary ropes. These defining moments have brought nations together and stoked feelings of collective pride, joy, and camaraderie among people hailing from a variety of cultural and ethnic traditions. In this investigation of 3,000 words, we revisit several of these historic events that went on to become significant milestones in the history of cricket. The triumph of India in the World Cup in 1983 and the astonishing draw score in the Test match between Australia and the West Indies in 1960 are two examples of the historical events that are dissected here, along with the tremendous effect these events had on national and international identities.

1. **The Opening Statements**
   The United Nations: Bonds Beyond Boundaries commemorated some of cricket's most iconic moments
   Cricket, which is frequently referred to as a gentleman's game, possesses the unique potential

   to unite nations and to transcend cultural, geographical, and political borders. The long and illustrious history of the sport is replete with famous moments that not only characterized games but also played an important role in the formation of the national identities of many countries. In this investigation of 3,000 words, we dig into some of these remarkable events in cricket that brought countries together and sparked a global sense of solidarity and celebration. These incidents have left an indelible stamp on the history of cricket and continue to resonate in the hearts of fans all over the world, from underdog victories to nail-biting ties and record-breaking feats.

2. **The Indian Team's Unbeatable Run in the 1983 Cricket World Cup**
   The year 1983 marked a turning point in the annals of cricket's long and illustrious history, and India's triumph in the Cricket World Cup was a significant factor in the formation of the country's character. It was the first time that a team other than the West Indies had won the event, and a young, vibrant team led by Kapil Dev raised the prized cup at Lord's to celebrate their victory. The triumph inspired a sense of national pride, cohesion, and aspiration among millions of Indians and reverberated throughout the country. It was a moment that went beyond the sport of cricket and heralded India's arrival on the international stage.

3. **The England victory against Australia in 1981, known as "The Miracle at Headingley"**

The Ashes series that is being played between England and Australia has created a lot of memorable moments, but the "Miracle of Headingley" stands out as one of the most iconic of them all. During the third and final match of the 1981 series, England, captained by Ian Botham, was attempting to avoid losing by scoring a target that appeared to be impossible to achieve.

An incredible triumph was achieved because to the amazing all-around performance of Botham, in addition to the courageous efforts of Bob Willis, who worked tirelessly. The amazing comeback served as a metaphor of resiliency and determination, bringing cricket fans in England closer together while also serving to celebrate the unpredictability of the sport.

VI. The Test That Ended in a Draw: Australia vs. the West Indies in 1960

The drawn-out test match between Australia and the West Indies in 1960 is widely regarded as one of the most exciting and important matches in the entire annals of cricket's long and illustrious history. The tension-filled last over, which was bowled by Wes Hall, epitomized the spirit of competitiveness while also highlighting the need of sportsmanship. The meeting between the two teams, which ended in a draw, was a demonstration of the intense rivalry as well as the mutual respect that exists between them. It brought fans from both countries together and solidified Test cricket's position as the most prestigious form of the sport.

V. India's Historic Victory in the Series Played in Australia, 2020-21

The latest and famous moment that gripped the cricketing globe was India's historic series win in Australia during the 2020-21 trip. This occasion occurred quite recently. In spite of the hurdles posed by injuries, quarantine restrictions, and a tough Australian team, India was able to clinch an amazing series triumph thanks to the illuminating leadership of Ajinkya Rahane. Fans of cricket came together to celebrate the unstoppable spirit of the game after India's victory, which was a representation of their country's resiliency and perseverance.

VI. Pakistan's Victory in the Cricket World Cup in 1992

The triumph of Pakistan against Australia and New Zealand in the Cricket World Cup in 1992 will forever be remembered fondly by fans of the game. The Pakistani cricket team bucked the odds to win the tournament while Imran Khan, a charismatic leader, was in charge. The victory became a point of national pride and brought the country closer together, despite the many different cultures and regions that exist inside the nation. It was a moment that brought Pakistanis together and demonstrated the nation's dominance in cricket on the international scene.

VII. The Exciting Concluding Moments of the ICC World Twenty20 Championship in 2007

The final match of the 2007 ICC World Twenty20, which was played between India and Pakistan, was a high-stakes battle that captivated the attention of millions of cricket fans around the world. The nail-biting conclusion, which resulted in India eking out a victory by a slim margin, exemplified the friendly sporting competition and mutual respect that exists between the two countries. It also offered as evidence of the capacity of cricket to bring people together in celebration of the sport, which served as a tribute to the sport's unifying effect.

VIII. England took against Australia in the eighth and final match of the Calcutta Cup in the year 1900

In 1900, England and Australia competed against each other for the Calcutta Cup. This match was a landmark event in the early history of test cricket. Clem Hill and Syd Gregory turned up outstanding efforts, which were largely responsible for Australia's tight victory in a game that was extremely close throughout. Cricket enthusiasts from all around the world came together to celebrate the spirit of rivalry and fraternity during the match, which took place in Calcutta and was watched by the British and Australian colonies.

IX. The Cinderella Story Behind Sri Lanka's Triumph at the 1996 Cricket World Cup

The stunning win that Sri Lanka achieved in the Cricket World Cup in 1996 was a watershed moment in the country's long and illustrious history of the sport. The group, inspired by Arjuna Ranatunga's leadership, was able to prevail against difficult competitors and win the tournament. A sense of national pride and solidarity was fostered as a result of the victory, which also served to underline Sri Lanka's rise as a formidable cricketing force and foster a sense of collective identity.

The most iconic moments in cricket are not only about the sport itself; rather, they are about the sense of togetherness, pride, and joy that they provide to nations and fans all around the world. These moments have crossed boundaries and cultures, bringing people together in celebration of the spirit of cricket. From historic victory at the World Cup to gripping tied Test matches, these moments have brought people together.

Cricket, as a unifying force, helps to influence the collective identities of nations while also helping to build experiences that will last a lifetime. It is a demonstration of the sport's ongoing ability to bring people together, honor differences, and motivate brilliance on the international stage. These classic moments have become an inextricable part of cricket's rich fabric, linking fans from all over the world and reminding us of the sport's ability to transcend linguistic barriers.

2.3 How cricket reflects cultural values and norms

Cricket, as a sport, acts as a reflection of the societal norms and values that are prevalent in the countries that enjoy playing it. This investigation of cricket and culture is 1500 words long and digs deep into the complex relationship between the two. It investigates how the sport reflects and reinforces the various identities, customs, and cultural norms of countries all over the world, including India, Australia, the West Indies, Pakistan, England, and more. We dissect the intricate ways in which cricket is woven into the fabric of national and international cultures, from the cultural rites and symbols that are linked with cricket to the way in which the sport develops a sense of community.

1. **The Opening Statements**
   The Way in Which Cultural Values and Norms Are Reflected in Cricket: An International Tapestry of Tradition and Identity
   The game of cricket, which is played all over the world and is considered by many to be a way of life for millions of people, is more than just a sport. It offers a lens through which we can grasp the intricate interplay of identity, heritage, and societal norms, reflecting the cultural values, customs, and traditions of the nations where it is passionately embraced. In this investigation of 1500 words,

we examine how the sport of cricket, which is a worldwide phenomenon, acts as a reflection of the distinct cultures of countries all over the world, including India, Australia, the West Indies, Pakistan, England, and many others. Cricket is a living narrative of tradition, passion, and the everlasting spirit of unity. This is because of the rituals and symbolism that are linked with the sport as well as the community that it generates.

2. **The Indian Cricket Team as an Example of Cricket's Role as a Cultural Ritual**

   Cricket is more than just a sport in India; it is also a cultural rite that brings together people of all different kinds of backgrounds. The activity is known for having its own set of traditions, which include chanting at stadiums and adhering to superstitions during competitions. Cricket, which is played all over India, is deeply ingrained in the country's culture and symbolizes the country's respect for its history, rituals, and symbols.

3. **Cricket and the so-called "Australian Way of Life"**

   It is common practice in Australia to refer to cricket as the "Australian way of life." The sport exemplifies the nation's affinity for the great outdoors, laid-back mentality, and profound connection to the natural world around it. Cricket exemplifies the laid-back and egalitarian nature of the Australian people while also showcasing their eagerness to take on new challenges.

4. **The West Indies: Cricket's Role in the Integration of Cultures**

   The diversified region of the West Indies, which is comprised of a number of different island nations, is home to a vibrant cricketing culture that reflects the blending of many aspects of other cultures. Cricket is a lively representation of Caribbean culture because of its distinctive fusion of cultural influences, which can be seen in aspects such as the music, the carnival-like atmosphere, and the style of play that is prevalent in the West Indies.

5. **The game of cricket and Pakistan's tenacious will to win**

   Cricket in Pakistan is a reflection of the nation's resiliency and capacity to find joy despite the country's difficult history and current conditions. The Pakistani culture emphasizes perseverance in the face of adversity, and cricket is an excellent vehicle for demonstrating this value. Cricket is a source of national pride and resilience, symbolizing the ability of the nation to prevail despite adversity.

6. **Cricket in England, a Game Steeped in History and an Example of True Sportsmanship**

   Cricket is a reflection of the traditions and sportsmanship of the country in which it was first played. The long and illustrious history of the sport in England serves as a symbol of the cultural legacy of the country and highlights the significance of honesty, fair play, and respect. For a long time, the sport of cricket has stood as a representation of traditional values and the ethos of the "gentleman's game."

7. **The Community That Cricket Fosters: An International Link**

   Cricket is one of the few sports that may create a sense of togetherness that is not limited by national boundaries or cultural norms. Fans from all over the world are able to form connections with one another via their passion for the sport, regardless of their cultural or religious differences. The worldwide community of cricket players and fans exemplifies the fundamental human need for connection, companionship, and the exchange of common experiences.

8. **A Mirror of Social Norms: Gender Roles and Inclusivity in Cricket**

The ever-evolving social standards of society are reflected in the perspective that cricket takes on gender and inclusiveness. The increasing participation of women in cricket draws attention to the shifting dynamics of gender equality in sports and underlines the power of sports to both reflect and change the norms of society.

Cricket is more than just a sport; the nations and communities that embrace it do so because it is a mirror of their cultural values, traditions, and societal conventions. It doesn't matter if you're in India, Australia, the West Indies, Pakistan, England, or any other region of the cricketing world; the sport represents a rich tapestry of identity, solidarity, and legacy wherever it's played. The sport of cricket captures the essence of what it means to be a part of a global culture that celebrates variety and shared enthusiasm. From the rituals and symbols that are connected with cricket to the sense of community that the sport generates, cricket encapsulates the essence of what it means to be a part of a global culture.

Cricket will always be a reflection of the values and conventions that make each culture unique, while simultaneously demonstrating the universal human yearning for connection and shared experiences as it continues to develop and captivate new generations.

This will be the case even as the sport continues to expand and capture new generations. Cricket is a great example of the enduring spirit of tradition, unity, and the celebration of the different cultures that help to make our globe a dynamic and linked tapestry of mankind. This spirit is exemplified by the game's ability to bring people from all over the world together to play the same game.

Chapter 3

Passion for the Game

Cricket is a sport that inspires a special and profound devotion in those who follow it, to the point where it is frequently compared to a religion for those who participate in it. In this investigation of three thousand words, we delve into the many layers of this enthusiasm, exploring the causes behind cricket's intense following, the emotional and cultural connections it forges, and the stories of cricketing passion from all corners of the world. The unshakeable commitment of fans in cricket-crazy countries like India, as well as the personal histories of players who live, breathe, and dream the game, are just two examples of the ways in which we uncover the heart of the enthralling passion that surrounds cricket.

1. **The Opening Statements**
   An In-Depth Look at Cricket's Unflinching Devotion to the Sport "Passion for the Game:"
   Cricket, which is frequently regarded as more than just a sport, possesses the unmatched potential to arouse a fiery and unmatched passion in the hearts of those who follow it. In the course of this investigation, which is three thousand words long, a deep dive is taken into the many dimensions of this devotion in an effort to discover the origins of cricket's steadfast following. We examine the essence of cricket's fascinating enthusiasm, from the emotional and cultural relationships it forms to the captivating stories of enthusiastic fans and players from around the world. Cricket is a sport that is played in a variety of countries throughout the world.

2. **Cricket's Devotees: The Diehard Supporters of the Game**
   Fans of cricket may be found all around the world, regardless of location or language barriers. In countries like India, which are completely obsessed with cricket, the enthusiasm for the game is through the roof. Cricket is a way of life for many people, as seen by the noisy cheering heard in stadiums and the emotional rollercoaster experienced by spectators during matches with high stakes.

We investigate the great commitment that fans have for the game of cricket, as well as the rituals that they participate in and the collective happiness that the game brings into their life.

3. **The Legendary Performers: Putting Their Hearts Into It**

Passion is more than just a feeling for the cricket players who represent their respective countries; it is a way of life for them. We dig into the personal narratives of renowned players who have committed their life to the game, detailing their adventures from modest beginnings to international stardom. These players are considered to be some of the best ever to play the game. The in-depth love of the game that drives professional cricket players like Sachin Tendulkar, Sir Vivian Richards, and Don Bradman is reflected in their backstories, which are told for the benefit of fans.

4. **The Role of Cricket in the Achieving of Goals**

Cricket provides a means to achieve one's goals in a number of nations, particularly those located on the Indian subcontinent. Because of their passion for cricket and the opportunities it may provide for them and their families to improve their lives, many young people who originate from disadvantaged families have the dream of becoming famous cricket players. The significance of cricket as a vehicle for social mobility and aspiration is examined via the personal narratives of cricket players who have triumphed against hardship to achieve greatness in their careers.

5. **Cricketing Rivalries Serve as a Playground for Passion**

Cricketing rivalries, such as the Ashes series between England and Australia or the contests between India and Pakistan, can elicit strong enthusiasm from fans of both countries. These competitions transcend the realm of sport and transform into occasions of national pride and enthusiasm, with fans having an emotional investment in the outcome of the game. We take a look at the background and significance of these rivalries, as well as the mental and emotional roller coaster that they offer to fans.

6. **The Emotional Rollercoaster: The Highs and Lows of the Experience**

The game of cricket can be an emotional rollercoaster, with highs and lows that put spectators' and players' dedication to the sport to the test. We dive into the agony of failure as well as the elation of success as we investigate the emotional roller coaster that the game of cricket puts its fans on during pivotal points in the match.

7. **The Contribution of Cricket to the Fields of Art, Music, and Culture**

The influence of cricket has spread beyond the playing field and into other areas of art, music, and culture. We examine how the sport of cricket has been ingrained in the cultural fabric of nations such as India and the West Indies via the lens of cricket-related music, literary and cinematic depictions of the game, and other forms of cricket-related artistic expression.

8. **Cricket's Grassroots Programs: Developing Players for the Next Generation**
   Cricket played at a grassroots level is extremely important for fostering a lifelong love of the sport. We take a look at the significance of cricket at the grass-roots level, focusing on how it fosters a passion for the game from a young age and influences the path that cricketing nations will take in the years to come.

9. **The Influence of Twenty20 Leagues on a Global Scale**

The introduction of Twenty20 leagues like the Indian Premier League (IPL) and the Big Bash League (BBL) has helped to further stoke the fires of fan enthusiasm for cricket. We investigate the business and entertainment spectacle that these leagues have become as well as the impact that these leagues have had on the landscape of cricket played around the world.

The love of cricket is more than just a feeling; it's a way of life for those who share it. Whether it's the supporters who paint their faces in the colors of their country, the players who shed sweat and tears for the game, or the young prospects who hope that cricket will be their ticket to a better life, the passion that surrounds cricket is a monument to the sport's ongoing appeal and significance.

Cricket has a way of bringing people together and forging connections that go beyond national boundaries and cultural norms. It sparks the spirit of unity and desire and provides a common language for fans from a variety of backgrounds and walks of life. The sport has an everlasting potential to bring people together, honor variety, and motivate excellence on the international stage, and despite the fact that the game is constantly changing and capturing the attention of new generations, its love has not waned. The passion that people have for cricket is a celebration of the human spirit, the pursuit of aspirations, and the communal delight that the sport offers to millions of people all over the world.

3.1 Cricket as a religion in some nations

In certain countries, cricket goes beyond the sphere of sports and becomes much more than just a game; it is elevated to the status of a religion. This investigation of the topic of cricket as a religion in countries such as India, Pakistan, Australia, the West Indies, and Sri Lanka spans 2,500 words and dives into the subject in length. Examining the deep-rooted cultural, social, and emotional links that give cricket its sacred status, examining the rituals and customs that are linked with the sport, and narrating the lives of those for whom cricket is not only a passion but a way of life are some of the topics that will be covered in this book.

1. **The Opening Statements**
   In Some Countries, Cricket Is Considered a Religion, Which Involves a Deep and In-Depth Devotion That Goes Far Beyond the Frontier
   In certain countries, cricket is elevated to the status of a religion, eliciting a level of devotion and zeal that goes far beyond the confines of a playing field. In this

investigation of two thousand and five hundred words, we set out on a quest to comprehend the phenomenon of cricket as a religion in nations such as India, Pakistan, Australia, the West Indies, and Sri Lanka. We dive into the cultural, sociological, and emotional linkages that raise cricket to a divine position. We also investigate the rituals and customs that are associated with the sport, and we relate the lives of individuals for whom cricket is not just a passion but also a way of life.

2. **The Divine Obsession That Is Cricket in India**

In India, cricket is more than just a pastime; it is an obsession that comes dangerously close to rivaling the zeal of religious practice. We investigate the long-standing ties that exist between cricket and Indian culture by focusing on the ways in which the game has been ingrained in the country's way of life, including its customs and practices. Attestations to the heavenly character of cricket include the deity-like status held by the renowned Sachin Tendulkar and the establishment of "cricket temples" in the form of venues such as Eden Gardens and Wankhede Stadium.

3. **Pakistan: Cricket and the Formation of a National Identity**

Cricket is a significant part of Pakistani culture, serving as a wellspring of national pride and identity and fostering a profound emotional connection among the population. We dig into the ways in which cricket represents togetherness and resiliency in a nation that has seen a great deal of adversity. The stories of cricketing superstars like Imran Khan, who made the transition from cricket to politics, highlight the significance of the sport in the social and political fabric of the nation.

4. **Australia: The Role of Cricket in Everyday Life**

The passion that Australians have for sports and the great outdoors is shown in the frequent use of the phrase "a way of life" to describe cricket. We investigate the historical and cultural significance of the Ashes series, as well as the influence that cricket has had on the identity of Australians, a country in which the sport is profoundly ingrained in the culture.

5. **The West Indies: Cricket's Role in the Integration of Cultures**

The West Indies, which is made up of several different Caribbean nations, is a great example of how cricket can function as a cultural melting pot by overcoming both geographical and cultural barriers. The music, the carnival-like atmosphere, and the energetic playing style of the West Indies all show a distinct fusion of cultural influences. Cricket is more than simply a sport; it is a festival that honors Caribbean culture and brings its people together.

6. **Sri Lanka: An Island Nation Obsessed with Cricket [and Tea]**

The devotion of the people of Sri Lanka to the game of cricket has given the sport the status of a religion. We investigate how cricket has brought the nation together and helped to cultivate a feeling of national pride, as well as the impact on Sri Lankan culture that has been exerted by cricketing icons such as Muttiah Muralitharan. The illustrious triumph at the Cricket World Cup in 1996 and the expansion of the sport at the grassroots level are both examples of the fervor with which Sri Lankans follow the sport.

7. **The Practices and Traditions of Cricket Regarding Its Role as a Religion**
   The practice of cricket as a religion is frequently accompanied by rituals and traditions that are frequently analogous to the tenets of traditional faiths. We investigate the beliefs that cricket is more than simply a game by looking at the various rituals, prayers, and superstitions that are practiced by both spectators and players.

8. **Cricket's Holiest Sites: the Hallowed Grounds**
   It is common practice to refer to grounds such as Lord's, the Melbourne Cricket Ground (MCG), and Eden Gardens as "cathedrals" of the sport of cricket. We investigate the significance of these iconic grounds and their part in the rise of cricket to the level of a religion in this article. These stadiums are more than just locations; for those who are devoted to cricket, they are places of religion.

9. **Personal Narratives: Taking Cricket in Through Every Portion of Our Being**

We discuss the individual experiences of people for whom cricket is not only a hobby but also a way of life. These tales demonstrate the breadth of feeling and commitment that the sport of cricket evokes in its followers, from spectators who make religious journeys to cricketing shrines to players who devote their entire lives to the sport.

For some people in the world, watching cricket is like to going to church; it is not only a sport, but also a way of life, a unifying force, and an expression of their national identity. A spiritual connection is formed between supporters of cricket and the sport through the various rituals, customs, and landmark grounds associated with the game.

Cricket continues to inspire religious devotion from new generations, despite the fact that the sport is constantly undergoing change and becoming more popular. Cricket is more than simply a game; for millions of people all over the world, it is a religion. This is a monument to the enduring ability of sport to unite people, celebrate variety, and inspire dedication beyond the boundary.

3.2 The fervor of cricket fans

Fans of cricket are famous for their unflagging zeal, boundless enthusiasm, and undying commitment to the sport. In this investigation of five thousand words' length, we delve deeply into the passion of cricket fans all over the world. We analyze the factors that contribute to their unshakeable commitment, from the thunderous screams heard in stadiums to the emotional rollercoaster felt during high-stakes matches, including both of these aspects. In addition to this, we investigate the significance of cricketing rivalries, the influence of technology on fan participation, and the role that cricket played in the formation of their cultural identity. We hope to gain a better understanding of the amazing world of cricket fandom through the use of stories, anecdotes, and in-depth analysis.

1. The Opening Statements
   The Passion of Cricket Supporters Is a Worldwide Phenomenon
   Cricket aficionados are a distinct subset of the population. Their devotion to the game goes much beyond simple adoration and develops into an entire way of life for them. The complexity of cricket fandom is the subject of this in-depth, 5000-word investigation, which aims to shed light on the subject. We look into the reasons behind their undying commitment, the emotional rollercoaster they feel during matches, as well as the cultural significance that cricket plays in their lives. We take a look at the unique world of cricket fandom, examining everything from the boisterous cheers heard in stadiums to the significance of cricketing rivalries.

2. **The Unwavering Devotion of a Cricket Supporter**
   Cricket enthusiasts are famously devoted to the sport they watch and play. We go into the mental and psychological underpinnings of this ardor to better understand it. Fans are emotionally invested in the outcomes of matches, experiencing a range of emotions from elation in the event of a victory to despair in the event of a loss. We dig into the traditions, superstitions, and friendships that contribute to the one-of-a-kind experience that is being a cricket fan.

3. **The Influence of the Stadium: Erupting Cheers and General Optimism**
   Attending a cricket match in person at a stadium provides a unique and un-forgettable experience. The atmosphere is unlike any other because of the high levels of energy, camaraderie, and sheer intensity of feelings. We investigate the relevance of the experience of being in a stadium, ranging from the "Barmy Army" in England to the "colorful crowds" in India.

4. **The Contribution of Cricket to the Formation of Cultural Identity**
   Cricket is more than just a sport; it is an integral component in the process of de-veloping the national cultural identities of countries. In this article, we dig into the ways in which the values, customs, and traditions of countries such as India, Australia, the West Indies, and Pakistan are reflected in the sport of cricket. Fans celebrate their heritage and find a way to show their sense of national pride via the sport of cricket.

5. **The emotional ups and downs that cricket spectators go through**
   During a match, the emotional landscape of a cricket fan can be likened to that of a rollercoaster. We take a look at the highs and lows that fans go through, from the joy of a six to the anguish of a dropped catch. The collective emotional

commitment in the game forges connections between players that are independent of national boundaries and cultural norms.

6. **The Cricketing Rivalries: Adding Fuel to the Passionate Fire**
Rivalries in cricket are an essential component of the game and help to stoke the passion of spectators. We look into the background and significance of some of the most famous rivalries in sports, such as the Ashes, India vs. Pakistan, and the wars between Australia and New Zealand that take place across the Tasman Sea. These competitions transcend the realm of sports and become into occasions of national pride and zeal.

7. **The Influence of Twenty20 Competitions Around the World**
T20 competitions like the Indian Premier League (IPL) and the Big Bash League (BBL) have completely changed the way fans interact with their favorite teams. We investigate how these leagues have given birth to a new generation of cricket fans and evaluate the influence these leagues have had on the landscape of cricket played around the world.

8. **The Relationship Between Technology and the Experience of the Fans**
The era of digital technology has brought about a change in the manner that fans interact with their favorite sports. We investigate the ways in which technology, like as live streaming and social media, as well as fantasy cricket and virtual reality, might contribute to improving the experience of the fans. Technology has enabled new forms of fan involvement and expression while also bringing spectators closer to the action of the game.

9. **The Slang of Fandom: Chants, Songs, and Artwork**
The zeal that the fans feel is communicated through art, chants, and songs. We investigate the unique methods in which fans show their appreciation for their favorite teams and games. These sentiments end up becoming ingrained in the culture of cricket in various forms, from well-known shouts such as "Sachin, Sachin" to artwork created by fans.

10. **The Outlook for the Popularity of Cricket**

The nature of being a fan shifts over time alongside the development of the sport. We talk about the future of cricket fandom, including topics such as the growth of women's cricket and the internationalization of the sport. The passion for cricket is still going strong despite the fact that fans are adapting to the changing circumstances.

The passion shown by cricket supporters is what keeps the sport alive, and they are the sport's essential source of vitality. Cricket is a global phenomenon that crosses national boundaries and cultural norms because of the emotional commitment, the cultural identity, and the everlasting devotion of its followers.

The zeal of cricket's fans has not waned even as the sport continues to win over new audiences and adapt to changing cultural norms and expectations. It is a monument to the enduring ability of sport to unite people, celebrate diversity, and inspire dedication beyond the boundary, which has turned cricket into more than simply a game but rather a way of life for millions of people all over the world.

3.3 The role of cricket in social bonding

The game of cricket is more than just a recreational activity; for millions of people all around the world, it is a way of life. It has the potential to reach beyond boundaries, bring people together, and establish social links that will stay. The purpose of this essay, which is 2500 words long, is to investigate the multidimensional function that cricket plays in building social interaction at all levels, from the local to the international level. We are going to look into the history, cultural significance, and impact that cricket has had on individuals as well as societies, stressing the fact that this sport draws people together like no other.

Before we begin:

Cricket is more than just a sport played on a field. It's a worldwide phenomenon that has the uncanny capacity to bring together people from all sorts of different places, cultures, and language backgrounds. Cricket has a way of creating connections and developing social bonds, regardless of whether it's a low-key game played in a nearby park or a high-stakes competition played on an international stage.

The history of cricket can be traced back to England in the 16th century, and throughout the course of several centuries, the game has made its way to numerous locations across the world, such as the Indian subcontinent, Australia, the West Indies, and even further afield. Each area has adopted the sport in its own special way, imbuing it with the various cultural and societal characteristics that are characteristic of that particular place. Because of this diversity, cricket has become a rich tapestry that goes across national boundaries and pulls people together.

The Power of Cricket to Bring People Together

Cricket has a long tradition of bringing together people from different backgrounds. It has been a means of bringing together people from various walks of life, often crossing social, economic, and racial barriers in the process. Because of the egalitarian aspect of the sport, players of all ages and origins are able to interact with one another on the field, which helps to cultivate comradery and friendship.

The Indian Premier League (IPL) is a prominent illustration of the function that cricket may play in the formation of social bonds. The Twenty20 cricket league that gets a lot of attention has turned into a cultural phenomenon in India. Fans from all walks of life come together to show their support for their favorite franchises in the Indian Premier League (IPL), which features teams that represent various towns and regions. The Indian Premier League (IPL) is not merely a cricket competition; rather, it is a celebration of India's variety as well as its togetherness.

The Ashes series against England is a cricket rivalry that extends far beyond the boundaries of a sport like cricket in places like Australia. It is a cultural phenomena that brings people from both countries together in a heated competition that is typically played in good fun. Even in the midst of intense competition, cricket has the power to forge social connections, as evidenced by the friendly banter and cama-raderie that has developed between fans of the two competing countries throughout the Ashes.

Cricket at the Local Level and Its Effects on Community

While international and professional cricket exemplifies the sport's ability to bring people together on a grand scale, grassroots cricket is an extremely important factor in the development of social links within small communities. People of various ages and from many walks of life are brought together via their participation in local cricket clubs and teams, which serve as the beating heart of many communities.

Cricket clubs offer individuals a venue in which they may participate in physical exercise, advance their skill set, and network with others. The comradery and friend-ships that are developed in circumstances like this often continue beyond the confines of the cricket pitch. These local activities, whether it be a group of friends playing a casual match on the weekend or children participating in junior cricket programs, establish a sense of connection and a common purpose for the community.

The local cricket club is not just a sports facility but also a social hub in many locations throughout the world where cricket is played. It is a location where people may gather to unwind, talk to one another, and build stronger links within the community. Individuals offer their time and knowledge to ensure that local cricket clubs are able to operate efficiently, which contributes to the widespread presence of the volunteer spirit in grassroots cricket.

The Importance of Cricket to National Identity

The sport of cricket has the potential to mold and form a nation's identity. It is more than just a sport in many nations; it is deeply ingrained in the national culture and has a significant place in the national legacy. Cricket matches, particularly those played against nations considered to be competitors, are known to inspire profound feelings of national pride and unity.

For example, cricket is far more than just a sport in India; it's actually a national obsession.

Cricket matches that feature the Indian national team are followed by millions of fans across the entire nation. The entire country grinds to a standstill whenever important competitions are taking place, such as the ICC Cricket World Cup, because people congregate in their homes, cafes, and other public locations to cheer on their side. Cricket has the potential to be a unifying force that can bridge geographical, linguistic, and cultural gaps, so contributing to the formation of a robust national identity.

In a similar vein, in Pakistan, where there is a wide variety of cultural traditions, cricket has been an important unifying force that has helped bring people together. In Pakistan, people of many provinces and walks of life are brought together by their shared love of cricket, which helps to strengthen their sense of national identity.

The influence of cricket on the formation of national identities is not unique to South Asia. Cricket has long been seen as a representation of regional pride in the West Indies. The cricket team known as the West Indies, which competes on behalf of a collection of Caribbean nations, has served as a source of motivation and togetherness. As a result of the team's success in the 1970s and 1980s, which is commonly referred to as the "Golden Age of West Indies Cricket," people from many islands were able to come together and further solidify their sense of collective identity.

The Importance of Cricket in Cultural Terms

It is impossible to overstate the significance of cricket to cultural traditions. It has had a profound impact on the cultures in which it is played, having an impact not only on art and music but also on literature and even language. The vocabulary of cricket and references to the sport may be found in a wide variety of cultural contexts, giving it a pervasive presence in everyday life.

The sport of cricket has appeared as a recurrent motif in the writings of a number of different authors throughout the history of the English language. Cricket has made its way into the works of renowned authors such as P.G. Wodehouse, Salman Rushdie, and C.L.R. James. These works of literature frequently employ cricket as a metaphor for life, drawing attention to the important life lessons that can be learned from the sport's emphasis on teamwork, strategy, and perseverance.

Additionally, cricket has made its way into the world of music. Songs that honor cricket's greats and those who have played the game are common in various nations throughout the world. Iconic songs like "Sachin, Sachin" in India and "The Cricket Song" in the West Indies have a strong connection with fans and are sung with a lot of passion during games. These songs not only aim to motivate listeners but also to bring to mind the profound relationship that exists between cricket and culture.

Cricket has been depicted in a wide variety of paintings and sculptures throughout the history of the art world. These works of art perfectly portray the majesty, talent, and excitement of the sport. The cultural relevance of cricket is frequently highlighted through the exhibition of works of art with a cricket subject at galleries and museums.

The Sport of Cricket as a Vehicle for Social Reform

Cricket has also been instrumental in promoting social change and resolving urgent concerns, which is an important part of the sport's history. Because it is capable of reaching a large number of people, it can serve as an efficient platform for bringing attention to vitally important social, political, and humanitarian concerns.

The anti-apartheid campaign in South Africa is one of the most significant examples of the role that cricket played in social transformation in that country. Due to the discriminatory laws that South Africa upheld throughout the apartheid era, the country was excluded from participation in international cricket. Cricket played a vital part in bringing attention to the injustice of apartheid, and it was via the sport that worldwide pressure was brought to bear on the government of South Africa to end the racist system.

Nelson Mandela, who would go on to become the first black president of South Africa, used the sport of cricket as a metaphor for national unity. He understood the power that sports may have to heal racial wounds and encourage unity among people of different backgrounds. After racial segregation in South Africa was abolished, Nelson Mandela's public endorsement of the national cricket team served as a potent symbol of the country's continued progress toward racial harmony and peace.

In recent years, cricket has served as a forum for discussions on topics such as mental health and gender equality. T20 leagues for women, such as the Women's Big Bash League (WBBL), as well as the Women's Cricket World Cup, have been essential in the advancement of women's cricket and the dismantling of gender stereotypes in the sport. Female cricketers have emerged as powerful role models in recent years, motivating younger girls and breaking established gender conventions.

The sport of cricket has also been utilized to bring attention to concerns pertaining to mental health, since a number of players have been transparent about the challenges they face in this area. This has resulted in a deeper understanding and acceptance of the issues that exist in society around mental health, as well as the significance of seeking assistance and support when necessary.

Cricket as a Tool of Diplomacy

The term "cricket diplomacy" refers to the important role that cricket plays in the process of

building diplomatic relations between countries. It has been utilized as a device for the purposes of de-escalating tensions, constructing bridges, and developing chances for communication and collaboration.

When India and Pakistan played each other in a cricket match, it became known as one of the most famous examples of cricket diplomacy. The competition between these two countries in the sport of cricket is fierce, and matches between them are watched by millions of people. On the other hand, there have been times when playing cricket has served as a tool to strengthen relations between two countries. Often referred to as "cricket diplomacy," the historic cricket series that India hosted against Pakistan in 2004 was considered as a step towards improving relations between the two countries.

In addition, cricket diplomacy has been utilized with regard to the situation in Afghanistan. Despite the fact that it was only recently established, the Afghan national cricket team has become a symbol of hope and solidarity in a country that has been torn apart by conflict.

The success of the Afghan national cricket team on the international stage has brought a sense of pride and excitement to the people of Afghanistan, transcending the country's ethnic and regional divides.

It was a momentous occasion for both Afghanistan and Pakistan when, in 2011, Afghanistan participated in its very first One Day International (ODI), which was contested against Pakistan. The purpose of the match was not simply to compete in cricket; rather, it was to demonstrate how sports have the power to unite people and advance the cause of peace.

Cricket and the Worldwide Spread of It

The popularity of cricket across the world has increased dramatically during the past several decades. The sport has now extended to many different parts of the world, but in the past it was more commonly linked with the countries that were part of the British Commonwealth. This globalization has not only resulted in an increase in the number of fans, but it has also made it possible to communicate and connect with people from other countries.

The International Cricket Council (ICC) is the organization that oversees cricket on a global scale and has been instrumental in advancing the globalization of the sport. Its name stands for the same thing. The International Cricket Council (ICC) is responsible for organizing a number of international competitions, such as the Cricket World Cup and the ICC World Twenty20, both of which feature the participation of teams from all over the world.

The globalization of cricket has resulted in a broad group of spectators and players that come from a variety of cultural and ethnic backgrounds. Players from countries that do not traditionally play cricket, like as Afghanistan, Nepal, and the Netherlands, have emerged on the world arena and take great delight in representing their respective nationalities. Cricket's potential to transcend national boundaries and foster world-wide togetherness is shown by the sport's rich diversity.

Cricket and Participation Among Young People

Cricket is a powerful tool for engaging young people and providing them with a sense of agency because of its one-of-a-kind appeal to this demographic. Young people can learn important life qualities including teamwork, leadership, discipline, and tenacity through participation in sports, which give a platform for such development.

Many nations have responded to the need to cultivate young talent and provide opportunity for personal development by launching youth cricket programs and initiatives.

These programs serve as a method of keeping young people involved in positive activities, especially in places where they may be vulnerable to social concerns such as substance misuse and delinquency. In addition, these programs serve as a means of keeping young people interested in positive activities.

The Indian Premier League (IPL), which was just mentioned previously, has proven to be particularly successful in attracting new talent and giving a stage for up-and-coming players to demonstrate their abilities. The success of the Indian Premier League has resulted in the rise of a new generation of young cricketers who are now recognized all over the world.

Young people can gain a feeling of purpose and belonging by participation in cricket, in addition to developing their existing skills. They get the opportunity to represent their towns and nations, which instills a powerful feeling of pride and gives them a sense of who they are as individuals.

Disputes and Obstacles to Overcome

Although cricket has a largely good influence on social connection and unity, the sport is not without its share of difficulties and debates. To guarantee that cricket continues to be a force for good in society, it is imperative that these problems be recognized and dealt with.

Corruption and the manipulation of matches are two of the most significant problems affecting cricket today. These immoral acts bring into question the legitimacy of the sport and weaken the faith that people have in it. Although the authorities and regulating organizations of cricket have been working relentlessly to eradicate match-fixing and spot-fixing, the problem still persists despite their efforts.

The fact that cricket can be played at a more elite level in some areas is another cause for concern. In nations such as India, where cricket is played by a huge number of people, there is a big divide between the chances that are presented to players in metropolitan areas and those that are presented to players in rural regions. This inequality can lead to brilliant players from less privileged backgrounds being underrepresented in the game, which is unfortunate.

Another obstacle is the mental and physical toll that playing professional cricket has on players. Both the strenuous schedule and the continuous travel can take their toll on their physical health, while the pressure to perform regularly can lead to concerns with mental health. Several cricket players have been candid about the challenges they have faced with their mental health, focusing emphasis on the significance of support and understanding in this area.

Another cause for concern is the effect that cricket has on the surrounding ecosystem. The building and upkeep of cricket stadiums, as well as the substantial travel that is associated with international cricket, have an impact on the environment. There are current efforts being undertaken to make cricket more sustainable and beneficial to the environment.

There is no denying the importance of cricket in the formation of social bonds. The sport of cricket brings people together, regardless of their nationality, culture, or language, and it does so in settings ranging from backyard cricket clubs to international competitions. It plays a role in the formation of national identities, provides a forum for social change, and functions as a diplomatic instrument. Cricket has a deep cultural significance that is reflected in literature, music, and other forms of art. Additionally, the sport is popular among young people and offers them opportunities for personal growth.

The benefits that cricket brings to society much outweigh any negatives associated with the sport, despite the fact that it is not without its share of problems and debates. It is possible that as the sport continues to globalize and progress, it will become an even more powerful force for unifying people and bringing about constructive change.

The enduring power of sports in our world is exemplified by the capacity of cricket to bring people together and strengthen the relationships that exist between them.

Chapter 4

Cricket and Politics

Cricket, also known as the "gentleman's game," has a lengthy and complex history that is intricately entwined with politics. This history dates back many decades. The sport, with its extensive global reach and passionate fan base, has repeatedly found itself embroiled in political narratives, functioning as a weapon for diplomacy, nationalism, and even protest. This is because the sport has a vast global reach and a passionate fan base. Within the scope of this three-thousand-word paper, we will investigate the intricate connection that exists between cricket and politics. More specifically, we will investigate the various ways in which governments, individuals, and organizations have used cricket to advance political objectives, mold national identities, and facilitate international interactions.

Before we begin:

Cricket, which is played all over the world in a variety of different cultures, has frequently been employed as a medium for political expression and participation. Because of the sport's widespread appeal, particularly in nations such as India, Pakistan, Australia, England, and the West Indies, political leaders and governments have found it to be an effective instrument for connecting with the general populace and reinforcing their political views through the medium of the sport. The junction between cricket and politics, on the other hand, is not always clear cut; it frequently raises problems about the ethical implications of utilizing sports for political benefit.

The Role of Cricket in the Expression of National Pride

The development of national pride and identity is one of the most crucial ways in which politics and cricket are inextricably intertwined. Cricket is a popular sport around the world, and in many of those nations, it serves as a symbol of national togetherness. Victories on the cricket field are frequently equated with successes at the national level.

For instance, in India, the success of the national cricket team is celebrated with fire and enthusiasm. Its accomplishments are frequently considered as a reflection of the country's ability to compete successfully on the international scene. The illustrious triumph of the Indian cricket team in the 1983 Cricket World Cup, which they achieved under the guidance of Kapil Dev, is commonly recognized as a defining event in India's rich history of athletic achievement. The victory not only resulted in the return of the illustrious trophy, but it also instilled a sense of national pride and unity, which will hopefully serve as a source of motivation for future generations of cricket players.

In a similar vein, cricket has been a significant contributor to huge levels of national pride in Pakistan. Despite the highs and lows it has experienced, Pakistan's national cricket team has been able to serve as a unifying force for its citizens, transcending political, ethnic, and geographical barriers. Celebrated as moments of national triumph, Pakistan's victories against archrivals such as India or Australia serve to reinforce the country's resiliency and power on the international scene.

Cricket has had a huge impact on the collective identity of Caribbean nations, particularly in the West Indies. This has been the case across the Caribbean. Not only did the success of the West Indies cricket team in the 1970s and 1980s cement the region's position as a powerhouse in cricket, but it also created a sense of regional pride and togetherness among the various nations that make up the Caribbean. This occurred throughout the time period of the 1970s and 1980s.

The game of diplomacy and cricket

Cricket has also been used as a diplomatic weapon, helping to improve bilateral relations between countries and facilitating conversation between them, which is especially important given the historically contentious nature of some of these partnerships. Different governments and leaders have taken advantage of the sport's ability to transcend political conflicts in order to start conversations and cultivate goodwill.

Between India and Pakistan is where we see one of the most famous examples of cricket's role in international diplomacy. The two nations, who are well-known for the political and military hostilities that have persisted between them for a significant amount of time, have frequently used cricket as a tool to establish communication and reduce diplomatic difficulties. Cricket matches between India and Pakistan, sometimes known as "cricket diplomacy," have been used by the leaders of both countries as occasions to participate in peaceful negotiations and encourage cultural relations.

Both India and Pakistan took part in a historic cricket series in 2004, which was dubbed the "Friendship Series," and it was considered as a key step in normalizing relations between the two nations. The games were more than just sporting activities; they were also meant to be symbolic of the desire for peace and healing between the two nations who are neighbors to each other.

In addition to this, cricket has been instrumental in the development of diplomatic ties between many nations. Despite the political disparities that exist between countries, the sport has been used as a tool to build bridges and strengthen ties between the countries.

The growth of diplomatic relations has been aided by the many different bilateral cricket tours and competitions that have served as forums for the sharing of cultural ideas and increased mutual comprehension.

Cricket and Demonstrations

Cricket has been used as a means of protest and resistance against repressive governments and social injustices. In addition to its significance in diplomacy and as a source of national pride, cricket has also played a role in international relations. Individuals and communities have been able to effectively push for political change and voice their disapproval via the sport, which has been a significant instrument in this regard.

During the time when apartheid was in place in South Africa, cricket was an important part of the resistance effort against the system. Due to its discriminatory policies, South African cricket was banned from international competition, which brought attention to the injustice of the apartheid system and mobilized global opposition to the dictatorship. The attempts of anti-apartheid activists, which included notable personalities such as Nelson Mandela, to boycott South African cricket further emphasized the discriminatory nature of the state and urged for its dismantlement.

In a similar vein, cricket has been utilized as a form of protest against the authoritarian policies of the government in Zimbabwe. The players and activists involved in the sport have used the platform provided by the sport to bring attention to violations of human rights and to call for political reforms. The fact that some international teams chose not to travel to Zimbabwe under the reign of Robert Mugabe is a glaring example of how sports can be used to confront authoritarian regimes and advance democratic ideals.

Politics and Bribery in the Sport of Cricket

Cricket has a long history of being used for political goals; yet, the sport has also been plagued by incidents of corruption and political involvement, both of which have given rise to severe worries about the sport's overall integrity. The connection between cricket's politics and its pervasive culture of bribery and other forms of dishonesty has harmed the sport's reputation and damaged spectators' and other stakeholders' faith in it.

There has been an issue of match-fixing and spot-fixing in cricket, in which players and officials have been discovered to alter the outcome of matches for the purpose of personal benefit or to serve the interests of third parties. This has been one of the most serious challenges that cricket has faced in recent years. Not only have these unethical activities degraded the image of the sport, but they have also raised questions about the role that political influence plays in defining the landscape of cricket.

Concerns have also been raised regarding the influence of politics in cricket's administrative structure. In certain nations, political leaders and officials in the government have abused their positions of power to improperly influence cricket boards, which has resulted in conflicts of interest and problems with governance. Because of this, there is frequently a lack of openness in the decision-making processes, partiality in the selection of teams, and improper management of financial resources.

The Indian Premier League, also known as the IPL, has had its fair share of controversy over issues of political meddling and corruption. The league has been plagued by allegations of match-fixing, conflicts of interest among team owners and administrators, and financial irregularities, which cast a cloud over the league's integrity and credibility.

Cricket and the Advancement of the Nation

Cricket, despite the many challenges it presents, has been an important factor in many

countries' efforts to foster national development and social togetherness. Cricket has been recognized as having the potential to be a catalyst for social change, and as a result, governments have begun to invest in the necessary infrastructure, training facilities, and youth development programs in order to harness the power of the sport for the benefit of society.

Young people in places like India, where cricket has a big following, have benefited from using the sport to teach them sportsmanship, discipline, and the importance of working together as a team. Opportunities for aspiring cricket players to perfect their skills and pursue a career in the sport have become available as a result of the establishment of cricket academies, training camps, and talent scouting programs.

Cricket has been used in Pakistan as a means of encouraging togetherness and resilience in a country that is facing a variety of socio-political issues. This has been one of the country's most significant contributions to the sport. Not only has the development of cricketing infrastructure, the introduction of domestic leagues, and the fostering of young talent helped to the growth of the sport, but it has also offered a source of hope and inspiration for the nation's youth. In other words, cricket has had a positive influence on the nation's youth.

In a similar vein, the sport of cricket has been crucial in the development of national pride and solidarity in countries such as Afghanistan and Bangladesh. The success of their respective national cricket teams has given the people a sense of identification and belonging, which has contributed to the strengthening of their nation's development and their sense of self-confidence.

The Internationalization of Cricket and Its Influence on Politics

The globalization of cricket, which has resulted in an increased presence of the sport on the international scene, has added additional aspects to the way in which politics and the sport interact with one another. International cricket competitions, such as the Cricket World Cup and the ICC World Twenty20, as well as bilateral series, have evolved into stages on which nations may exhibit their best cricket players and improve their standing in the eyes of the international community.

The diplomatic opportunities that are given by hosting international cricket events have been acknowledged by governments and leaders around the world. A nation's standing in the world, as well as its ability to entice international investment and tourism, can both be improved by successfully hosting a big cricket tournament. For instance, the West Indies hosted the ICC Cricket World Cup in 2007, which brought together teams and spectators from all over the world. This event was a source of tremendous pride for the region and also had a significant impact on the economy of the region.

There have been political repercussions as a result of the expanding political clout of the Indian Premier League (IPL) and other franchise-based Twenty20 leagues. The Indian Premier League in particular has been successful in luring substantial investments and sponsorship deals, and as a result, prominent politicians, celebrities, and business magnates have become owners of IPL teams. This mixing of politics and cricket has given rise to concerns over potential conflicts of interest and excessive influence on the sport's management. [Cricket and politics] have become increasingly intertwined in recent years.

In international cricket, some of the challenges and controversies include:

Politics have been the source of more than its fair share of controversy and difficulties in the game of international cricket. The imbalance of power among the cricketing nations, also known as the "Big Three" issue, is consistently cited as one of the most contentious concerns in the sport as a whole. In 2014, the Board of Control for Cricket in India (BCCI), the England and Wales Cricket Board (ECB), and Cricket Australia (CA) signed an agreement that gave them a larger portion of the money and the right to make decisions pertaining to international cricket. This agreement was known as the International Cricket Council (ICC) Agreement. This action was met with criticism from other nations that play cricket, which led to worries regarding the impact of these big boards on the governance of the sport.

The protection and safety of players participating in international cricket matches has also been a sensitive topic. This is due to the fact that political turmoil and the fear of terrorism in certain locations have raised questions about the viability of holding international matches. As a result of safety concerns, a number of international tours and tournaments have either been scrapped entirely or relocated to different locations.

The employment of technology in international cricket, specifically the Decision Review System (DRS), has sparked political debates. Some teams have enthusiastically embraced the use of technology to evaluate the judgments made by the umpires, while other teams have raised doubts about the practice, citing concerns about the technology's accuracy and reliability.

Cricket and the Politics of Gender

Cricket has frequently been a medium through which gender politics have been reflected and affected, particularly in the context of women's cricket. The campaign for female cricketers' right to respect, equality, and chances has been going on for a very long time, despite the fact that gender bias and discrimination are still common in many countries that play cricket.

In recent years, women's cricket has been increasingly popular as a result of the Women's Cricket World Cup and numerous Twenty20 leagues, both of which offer a stage upon which female cricket players can demonstrate their talents. Despite this, there are still gender gaps in terms of income, access to facilities, and opportunity, which is reflective of greater gender inequalities in society.

The #MeToo movement has also made its mark in the sport of cricket, with charges of sexual harassment and gender-based discrimination rising to the forefront of the conversation. These occurrences have sparked conversations about the necessity of creating a cricketing atmosphere that is more egalitarian and welcoming to all players.

Cricket and the Activism of Politicians

A few members of the cricketing community have leveraged their public profile to get involved in political action and fight for social justice. They were able to campaign for change and raise awareness about important issues by using the sports field, which provided them with a venue unlike any other.

For instance, in recent years, cricket stars like England's Jofra Archer and West Indies' Darren Sammy have taken advantage of their visibility to speak out against racism and support social justice. They have engaged in conversations about racial equality and justice, and they have taken a knee in support of the Black Lives Matter movement. By doing so, they have brought attention to these important problems within the cricketing community.

The connection between cricket and politics is one that is fraught with contradictions and convoluted. It cannot be denied that cricket plays an important part in its position as a symbol of national pride, a weapon for diplomacy, a stage for protest, and a method of supporting national progress. It has the ability to unite people, to bridge political divides, and to form the identities of nations.

On the other hand, the influence of politics in cricket has not always been for the better. Concerns have been expressed concerning the integrity of the sport as well as the governance of it due to problems with corruption, undue influence, and conflicts of interest. In addition, the sport continues to face challenges stemming from gender inequality, as well as difficulties relating to security, technology, and power imbalances among the nations that play cricket.

The sport of cricket is intrinsically related to political narratives and agendas due to the fact that it is played all over the world, has a large fan base, and exerts a significant amount of influence. Despite the fact that this relationship has the potential to be exploited for positive change, it still takes monitoring to ensure that cricket continues to be a force for unity, growth, and social justice.

The intricate connection that exists between politics and cricket highlights how important it is for the governance of the sport to adhere to high standards of ethics, openness, and accountability. Cricket's enduring appeal and influence on the world stage make it a powerful instrument for promoting political and social change; but, its potential can only be achieved when it is used properly and ethically to benefit society as a whole. Cricket's worldwide popularity and influence on the world stage make it a powerful tool for promoting political and social change.

4.1 The intersection of cricket and politics

Cricket, which is frequently seen as more than just a sport, has a profound and long-standing confluence with politics on both the national and international levels. Cricket, a sport that commands a passionate following and furious engagement, has often found itself embroiled in political narratives, functioning as a weapon for diplomacy, nationalism, and even protest. This is because cricket is a game that demands a passionate following and fervent involvement. This article, which is two thousand and five hundred words long, will delve into the historical, cultural, and modern aspects of cricket's intersection with politics, as well as analyze the impact that this intricate relationship has had on the landscape of both the sport and the political sphere.

Before we begin:

The connection between politics and cricket has a long and complicated history that spans multiple continents and civilizations. The popularity and resonance of the sport have frequently led to its utilization as a representation of national pride, a tool for diplomatic endeavors, and a stage for public demonstrations. Nevertheless, there has been disagreement and difficulty associated with this interaction. In order to gain a full comprehension of the complex nature of the relationship that exists between cricket and politics, one must first conduct an exhaustive study of the development of cricket throughout history and the political landscape of today.

Colonial Origins and the Formation of National Identity in Historical Context

The British Empire is credited with introducing and popularizing cricket throughout the colonial era, which is when the sport's beginnings can be traced back to. As a direct consequence of this, the game eventually became deeply ingrained in the social fabric of a great number of countries that the British had previously ruled as colonies. The impact of colonialism on the growth and spread of cricket, which in turn shaped the cultural and political significance of the game in these areas, was long-lasting and significant.

Cricket has become an inextricable component of the national identities of several nations,

including India, Pakistan, Australia, and the West Indies. It is a symbol of the nations' common history and legacy. The legacy of colonialism also contributed to the development of intricate power dynamics inside the sport, which in turn influenced the sport's governance, administration, and structural makeup.

The game of cricket as a representation of national pride and cohesiveness

The function that cricket plays as a symbol of national pride and solidarity is one of the most notable connections that can be made between the sport and politics. The success of a country's national cricket team is frequently lauded since it is seen as a reflection of the collective identity and accomplishments of that country. When a team wins a tournament that is played on a global scale, it is celebrated as a moment of triumph that is unaffected by political, ethnic, or regional boundaries.

For example, the victory of the Indian cricket team in important events such as the ICC Cricket World Cup and the ICC World T20 have been celebrated all over the country with a great deal of fervor and enthusiasm. These victories have not only contributed to the growth of the nation's rich sporting heritage, but they have also contributed to the growth of a sense of national pride and solidarity among India's incredibly diverse population.

In a similar vein, cricket has been a unifying force in Pakistan, bringing together individuals from a variety of provinces and communities under the banner of the national team. The accomplishments of the Pakistan national cricket team have been a tremendous source of pride and happiness for the country's population, helping to cultivate a feeling of communal identity and purpose.

The Power of Sport in International Relations, Exemplified Through the Game of Cricket

Cricket has been used on numerous occasions as a diplomatic tool, which has contributed to the development of discussion and improved ties between nations.

Because of its potential to transcend political tensions, sport has been used by governments and leaders to start conversations and foster cultural exchanges. This is especially true in the context of historically fraught ties, where relations have been tense in the past.

The "cricket diplomacy" that has taken place between India and Pakistan is a perfect example of how the sport can be utilized to alleviate tensions and encourage peaceful contact between nations at odds with one another. The scheduling of cricket matches between the two countries has frequently provided opportunities for the leaders of both nations to interact with one another and debate issues of common interest, so fostering an environment that is conducive to conversation and cooperation between the two nations.

In a similar vein, the sport of cricket has been significant in fostering cross-national understanding and cooperation. The establishment of diplomatic relations and the cultivation of goodwill between nations have both been aided by the proliferation of bilateral cricket tours and competitions, which have served as forums for the interchange of cultural ideas and increased mutual comprehension.

The Game of Cricket as a Vehicle for Protest and Social Transformation

Cricket has been used both as a forum for protest and as a vehicle for social change in addition to the function it plays in diplomacy. The activity has served as a forum in which individuals and communities have been able to express their disagreement with governmental systems and call for greater social equality and reform.

Cricket became a focal point for the anti-apartheid movement in South Africa during the apartheid era, with worldwide boycotts and rallies drawing attention to the discriminatory policies of the apartheid regime. During this time, cricket was a popular sport in South Africa. The actions of anti-apartheid activists, combined with the backing of the international cricket community, played a vital role in calling into question the legitimacy of the apartheid government and pushing for its removal from power.

In a similar vein, cricket has been used as a form of resistance against repressive governments in Zimbabwe. Players and activists have leveraged the sport to bring attention to violations of human rights and political injustices. The fact that foreign cricket teams have chosen to withhold their participation in tours of Zimbabwe is evidence of the ability of the sport to serve as a vehicle for political protest and activism.

Governance and bribery in the context of cricket and political power

Political power dynamics have had an impact on the administration of cricket, which has resulted in instances of political meddling and disputes. Political leaders and officials in government have frequently used their positions of power to push their influence on cricket boards, which has frequently resulted in conflicts of interest as well as difficulties in governance and administration.

Match-fixing and spot-fixing are examples of unethical practices that degrade the image of cricket and threaten to undermine its popularity. The problem of corruption in cricket has also been a significant source of worry. The intersection of politics and bribery has led to concerns over the openness and accountability of cricket's governance, as well as to demands for more stringent regulatory systems and moral guidelines.

The Internationalization of Cricket and the Political Consequences of This Fact

Cricket's reach and influence have increased as a result of the sport's increased globalization, which has opened up new avenues for the sport's confluence with politics. Cricket competitions that take place on a worldwide scale, such as the ICC Cricket World Cup and the several Twenty20 leagues that have sprung up in its wake, have given nations the chance to demonstrate their prowess and raise their profile on the international stage.

The Indian Premier League (IPL) has become a worldwide sensation that has attracted large investments and sponsorships from prominent political figures, celebrities, and business magnates. Because of the presence of these powerful figures, questions have been made concerning the extent to which the administration and management of the sport are influenced by political and economic interests.

Gender Dynamics and Sociopolitical Issues Bring About a Host of Difficulties and Controversies

The gender dynamics of society have been mirrored in and impacted by cricket, most notably in the context of women's cricket. In spite of the fact that women's cricket is becoming increasingly popular, there are still significant gender gaps in terms of salary, facilities, and opportunity, which brings to light broader issues of gender inequality in society.

The sport has also struggled with sociopolitical issues, including as worries about safety, the application of technology in decision-making, and power imbalances between cricketing nations. While discussions over the utilization of technology have brought to light the requirement for a balanced approach to integrating innovation into the game, the possibility of staging international matches in certain regions has been called into question due to the presence of political upheaval and security issues in such areas.

The relationship between cricket and politics has a long and storied history, and it has had a significant impact on the cultural, social, and political landscapes of a number of countries. In spite of the fact that the relationship between the two is frequently intricate and multi-layered, it serves to highlight the significant role that sports play in forming national identities, promoting diplomatic relations, and lobbying for social change. However, because of the difficulties and issues involved with this confluence, the world of cricket needs to take a more watchful approach to ensuring openness, ethical governance, and the promotion of inclusivity and equality. Stakeholders may work toward leveraging the good potential of cricket as a unifying and transforming force in the global political arena if they recognize the complexity and nuances of this relationship.

4.2 How cricket has been used for diplomatic purposes

Cricket, which is frequently considered to be more than just a sport, has played a role in diplomatic relations between nations that is both distinctive and powerful. As a result of the sport's ability to transcend political boundaries and bring people together, diplomacy and international engagement can make effective use of the sport as a potent tool. In this essay of 1000 words, we will investigate how cricket has been utilized for diplomatic reasons, looking at historical examples, the impact that cricket has had on international relations, and the role that it has played in bridging the gap between nations.

Before we begin:

In several instances, the sport of cricket has been utilized as a vehicle for advancing diplomatic efforts and maintaining friendly relations between nations. Because of its widespread appeal and reach over the world, the sport offers world leaders and governments a common ground on which to participate in friendly rivalry and diplomatic discussion. Cricket matches and tournaments provide opportunity for nations to interact with one another, cultivate partnerships, and advance international understanding. In this article, we will investigate how cricket has been used for diplomatic objectives in a way that has led to improved relations between countries and increased international collaboration.

The Role of Cricket in India's and Pakistan's Attempts at Diplomacy

The cricket matches played between India and Pakistan are widely regarded as one of the most illustrious examples of cricket being utilized for diplomatic objectives. The political tensions and conflicts that have arisen as a result of this rivalry between these two states are well-documented. Cricket, on the other hand, has frequently used as a medium through which to commence calm discourse and ease diplomatic strains.

In 1987, General Zia-ul-Haq, who was serving as President of Pakistan at the time, traveled to Jaipur, India, to see a cricket match between India and Pakistan.

This historic visit was considered as a significant diplomatic gesture and a step towards normalizing relations between the two countries. It was also seen as an important step towards normalizing relations between the two countries. The cricket match was much more than just a sporting event; it was also a venue for diplomatic engagement and a symbol of goodwill between the two countries.

In 2004, India and Pakistan participated in what was known as a "Friendship Series" of cricket matches. These matches were considered as another diplomatic move to reinforce the two countries' existing connections to one another. The series was used as a backdrop for political officials from both countries to engage in conversations and promote cultural exchanges, which contributed to an environment that was more cooperative and peaceful.

Cricket's Role in International Relations and the Caribbean

The promotion of regional unity and cooperation in the Caribbean has also received a boost from the cricket diplomacy that has taken place. The cricket team known as the West Indies, which is comprised of players from a number of countries in the Caribbean, has become a symbol of regional pride and unity.

The exploits of the West Indies cricket team in the 1960s and 1970s served as a unifying force for the Caribbean nations. This was especially true during those decades when the team was at the pinnacle of its success. Not only did the success of the West Indies cricket team cement the region's image as a powerhouse in the sport of cricket, but it also strengthened a sense of regional pride and togetherness among the various nations that make up the Caribbean.

There have been numerous opportunities for diplomatic interaction at cricket matches featuring the West Indies because leaders and dignitaries from a variety of Caribbean nations frequently attend West Indies matches. The leaders of the Caribbean have been able to come together thanks to the sport, which has helped to strengthen the concept of regional togetherness and cooperation.

India and Australia Can Communicate Better Thanks to Cricket

The game of cricket has also been instrumental in bridging the gap that has long existed between India and Australia. The cricket competition between the two countries has historically been fierce, characterized by heated matches and fervent support from both sides of the field. Nevertheless, the sport has opened doors for diplomatic exchanges between the two nations, which has helped to improve the overall state of the two-nation relationship.

After the end of World War II in 1948, the legendary Australian cricketer Sir Don Bradman extended an invitation to the Indian cricket team to tour Australia.

This visit consisted of more than simply a cricketing back-and-forth; rather, it was viewed as a diplomatic attempt to improve the friendship that exists between the two countries. It was an encouraging development in the early stages of India and Australia's diplomatic engagement with one another.

The subsequent cricket tours and matches between the two countries have continued to serve as chances for cultural exchange and diplomatic interaction. The participation of world leaders in high-profile series and tournaments has served as a forum for them to engage in bilateral discussions and advance diplomatic relations, all while promoting a shared passion for the sport.

Diplomacy through Cricket in South Asia

The use of cricket as a tool for diplomatic relations has spread to additional South Asian nations. In recent years, India and Sri Lanka's diplomatic ties have been strengthened thanks in part to the contribution of cricket. Cricket was used as a tool of diplomacy between India and Sri Lanka in 1991, following a particularly severe phase in the countries' ties with one another. During his trip to Sri Lanka, Indian Prime Minister Rajiv Gandhi attended a cricket match in Colombo, which he used as an opportunity to deliver a message of friendliness and brotherhood. The purpose of the visit was to build stronger diplomatic ties between the two countries and to encourage reconciliation between them.

The people-to-people diplomacy between India and Bangladesh has been helped along in no small part by the sport of cricket. Both countries have been able to come closer together and learn more about one another's culture thanks to the sport of cricket, which is played internationally. The cricket matches that take place between India and Bangladesh are attracting a lot of attention and are being viewed as potential opportunities for diplomacy.

The sport of cricket and international relations

Cricket has also been used as a tool in international diplomacy, helping to bridge the gap between different nations and regions. The International Cricket Council (ICC), which acts as the regulatory body of cricket on a global level, has played an important role in fostering diplomatic relations between countries that participate in cricket. Tournaments hosted by the International Cricket Council (ICC), such as the ICC Cricket World Cup, have allowed nations hailing from a variety of locations to participate in diplomatic conversations and advance the cause of global cooperation.

The International Cricket Council (ICC) hosts worldwide events that attract dignitaries, political leaders, and cricket fans from all around the world.

These competitions act as a forum for the exchange of cultural traditions, the advancement of diplomatic ties, and the construction of diplomatic bridges between countries.

The Use of Cricket as an Instrument of Soft Power Diplomacy

Cricket is frequently seen as an instrument for soft power diplomacy that governments can utilize. Joseph Nye is credited with coining the term "soft power," which describes a nation's potential to influence other nations through its culture, values, and other non-coercive ways. Cricket is a useful tool for countries to use as part of their soft power strategy to promote their culture, values, and identity to the rest of the world.

Cricket has been used by countries such as India to increase their global influence by capitalizing on the sport's "soft power." Not only has the Twenty20 cricket competition known as the Indian Premier competition (IPL), which is built on franchises, increased the sport's popularity, but it has also projected India's economic and cultural power. Because of its success in luring players from other countries, investors, and spectators from all over the world, the Indian Premier League (IPL) has emerged as an important instrument for bolstering India's soft power on the international stage.

The Obstacles to Be Confronted in Cricket Diplomacy

Cricket diplomacy may have a track record of success in advancing diplomatic ties, but that does not mean it is without its share of obstacles. Cricket is known to be fraught with political complexity and sensitivities, both of which can occasionally give rise to disputes and tensions.

For instance, in the sport of cricket, diplomatic ties have occasionally been strained due to issues with the scheduling of matches, the selection of venues, and the cancellation of tours. Cricket tours have either been rescheduled or canceled due to safety concerns and the possibility of interruptions, which has a negative impact on diplomatic efforts and on the connections that exist between countries.

The disparities in power relations among cricket-playing nations, commonly referred to as the "Big Three" issue, have also produced conflicts inside the sport, raising questions about the fairness and inclusivity of the governance of international cricket.

The game of cricket has been used as a potent and successful instrument in the process of developing diplomatic relations between nations. The ability of sport to transcend political barriers and bring people together has resulted in new chances for conversation, cultural exchange, and the advancement of goodwill.

The historical examples of cricket diplomacy, such as those between India and Pakistan, India and Australia, and in the Caribbean, demonstrate the sport's potential as a form of diplomatic interaction. Historically, cricket has been played between India and Pakistan, India and Australia, and in the Caribbean. Cricket has also been instrumental in fostering regional solidarity and collaboration in South Asia and the Caribbean. This has been the case particularly in South Asia.

The International Cricket Council (ICC) has been instrumental in expanding cricket's function as a tool for international diplomacy, which has further strengthened cricket's significance as a diplomatic instrument. The ability of countries to showcase their cultural and economic prowess to the rest of the world has been made possible by the "soft power" of cricket, as shown through leagues such as the Indian Premier League (IPL).

Despite its widespread popularity, cricket diplomacy continues to struggle with issues with scheduling, safety concerns, and power disparities within the sport. In light of these issues, it is more important than ever for international cricket to have governance that is open and inclusive.

4.3 Controversies and political influences on the game

In spite of cricket's reputation as a "gentleman's game," the sport's lengthy history has been marked by a number of contentious debates and political interventions. The sport has a long reputation of sportsmanship and fair play, but it has also been plagued by incidences of corruption, political involvement, and issues in governance. In this essay of 1000 words, we will look into some of the most prominent controversies and political influences on the game of cricket, exploring the impact that these factors have had on the sport's integrity and governance as a result of these factors.

Before we begin:

The sport of cricket, which has strong historical roots and a following all over the world, has been confronted with a wide variety of difficulties due to controversies and political pressures. These problems have included everything from political influence in the management of the sport to scandals including allegations of corruption. In order to protect cricket's honor and ensure its continued success in the future, it is essential to gain an understanding of the impact that these scandals and political pressures have.

Scandals involving Match-Fixing and Spot-Fixing

The match-fixing and spot-fixing scandals were among the most major issues that rocked the world of cricket.

Spot-fixing refers to the manipulation of particular events or moments that take place within a match, as opposed to match-fixing, which refers to the manipulation of the outcome of an entire match. These unethical tactics have had a detrimental effect on the sport's integrity, which in turn has had a long-lasting effect on the reputation of cricket.

The incident involving South African captain Hansie Cronje and match-fixing in 2000 brought the topic to the forefront of public consciousness. Cronje's admission that he had accepted money from bookies in exchange for manipulating matches has raised worries about the frequency of activities like these in the sport of cricket. Cronje was banned from playing cricket as a direct result of the incident, which also brought attention to the urgent requirement for more strict anti-corruption measures inside the sport.

In a similar vein, the cricketing world was rocked to its core by the spot-fixing scandal that unfolded in 2010 and involved Pakistani cricketers Salman Butt, Mohammad Asif, and Mohammad Amir. The players were judged to be guilty of participating in a spot-fixing scam that was orchestrated by bookies, which involved bowling purposeful no-balls. Not only did the incident result in lengthy suspensions for the players, but it also brought up doubts regarding the susceptibility of cricketers to outside influences.

As a result of these controversies, the International Cricket Council (ICC) decided to create the Anti-Corruption and Security Unit (ACSU) in order to address the widespread problem of corruption in cricket. Since then, the ACSU has been instrumental in both the investigation and prosecution of those implicated in corrupt activities, as well as the education of players, officials, and other stakeholders about the dangers associated with corruption.

Administration of Cricket Containing Conflicts of Interest

The incidents involving match-fixing are only one example of the political impact on cricket. Political meddling and conflicts of interest have frequently had a negative impact on the ability of cricket boards and organizations to manage themselves effectively. In several nations, political leaders and government officials have abused their positions of power to impose an undue influence on the administration of cricket, which has led to difficulties with governance.

One of the most prominent cricket organizations in the world, the Board of Control for Cricket in India (BCCI), has been embroiled in a number of issues linked to political intervention and conflicts of interest. Because of the BCCI's reputation for maintaining tight relationships to a wide range of prominent people and political figures, there have been instances when questions have been raised regarding the organization's commitment to transparency and impartiality in its decision-making.

Conflict of interest difficulties have developed in cricket administration, with individuals having positions both in cricket organizations and other business or political activities. Because of this, issues have been raised about the impartiality of cricket boards and the possibility that decision-making can be influenced by elements from the outside.

The Controversy Surrounding the "Big Three" in International Cricket

Over the course of the last several years, political forces have begun to have an effect on the power structure in international cricket. The problem that came to be known as the "Big Three" controversy brought to light disparities in power and revenue-sharing arrangements among the nations that play cricket.

In 2014, the cricket governing bodies of India, England, and Australia all signed a deal that gave them a larger portion of the ICC's revenue as well as a greater say in the organization's decision-making process. Other countries who play cricket voiced their disapproval of this plan because they believed it would allow the "Big Three" to increase their dominance at the expense of the other countries.

The controversy surrounding the "Big Three" sparked concerns over the inclusiveness and fairness of the governance of international cricket. One sort of political maneuvering that was considered as disadvantageous to smaller nations and contradicted the values of equality and collaboration in cricket was the effect that large cricket boards had on the administration of the sport.

The debate ultimately resulted in the International Cricket Council (ICC) revising its governance model in an effort to correct these inequities and establish a system that is fairer in terms of the distribution of revenue and the making of decisions.

Worries about safety and upheaval in the political system

The game of international cricket has been significantly impacted, not only by safety concerns but also by political instability. Because of ongoing hostilities or political unrest, the staging of international matches in certain places has become difficult or dangerous. As a result, fewer matches are being played there.

For instance, Pakistan has had to deal with a number of security issues, which has caused international teams to decline the opportunity to tour the country. The terrorist attack that took place in Lahore in 2009 on the Sri Lankan cricket team was a defining moment in the sport of cricket because it brought to light the dangers that come with competing in areas where there is political unrest and the threat of terrorism.

Concerns were also raised over the possibility of international matches being played in Zimbabwe as a result of the country's political climate. Several international teams decided not to travel to Zimbabwe because they were concerned about the political climate there as well as the safety of the players and officials.

The rescheduling or cancellation of international cricket tours owing to safety concerns has had a negative influence on the sport's ability to reach new audiences throughout the world, and it has prompted questions about whether or not it is even possible to stage matches in areas that are experiencing political instability.

Application of Technology to the Process of Decision-Making

Politics has played a role in shaping debates regarding the application of technology in cricket, which has contributed to the sport's reputation for controversy surrounding this topic. The employment of technology to examine on-field umpiring decisions through a process known as the Decision examine System (DRS) has been the subject of debate within the cricketing world.

Some teams have welcomed the DRS, regarding it as a good instrument for ensuring fair play and accuracy in decision-making. They see it as a valuable tool for ensuring fair play and accuracy in decision-making. On the other hand, some individuals have voiced concerns regarding its accuracy and reliability, which has resulted in discussions and arguments regarding its application.

The implementation of new technologies in cricket has prompted speculation over the extent to which political power plays a role in the sport's administration and the decision-making process. Occasionally, the alignment of cricket boards and nations on this topic has been influenced by external causes, which has resulted in varied viewpoints on the incorporation of technology into the game.

The Indian Premier League and Its Influence on Politics

Political influences and scandals have not been absent from the Indian Premier League (IPL), which is one of the most watched and financially lucrative Twenty20 leagues in the world. Political personalities, celebrities, and business magnates have all become team owners in this league, which has resulted in huge investments and sponsorship deals being secured.

Because of the participation of influential people in the Indian Premier League (IPL), worries have been raised regarding the possibility of conflicts of interest and excessive political influence on the league's administration and management.

Concerns regarding the transparency and impartiality of decision-making processes within the Indian Premier League (IPL) have arisen on occasion as a result of the political connections and affiliations of team owners.

The sport of cricket has been significantly altered as a result of a number of contentious issues and political factors. The integrity of the sport has been harmed as a result of numerous incidents involving match-fixing and spot-fixing, which spurred the adoption of anti-corruption laws. Concerns regarding the administration of cricket's transparency and impartiality have been brought up as a result of concerns with conflicts of interest.

The "Big Three" issue brought to light inequities in the governance of international cricket, which in turn led to reforms aimed at making the system more equitable. The global reach of cricket has been hampered as a result of scheduling conflicts brought on by political turmoil and security concerns at international tournaments.

The application of technology, in particular the DRS, has given rise to disputes that are impacted by the dynamics of politics. Concerns have been expressed over potential conflicts of interest and political affiliations among IPL club owners as a result of the success and influence of the league.

Chapter 5

Cricket and Gender

In recent years, cricket has seen considerable changes, with an increasing emphasis on encouraging gender inclusion and equality. Traditionally, cricket has been perceived as a male-dominated sport. Cricket has experienced a spectacular rise in the popularity and recognition of women's cricket, as well as an increased focus on resolving gender imbalances within the sport. Despite its historical associated with masculinity, cricket has seen a remarkable rise in the popularity and recognition of women's cricket. This three-thousand-word essay will present a detailed examination of the impact that cricket has had on gender dynamics, analyzing its historical backdrop, the development of women's cricket, the obstacles faced by female cricketers, initiatives for gender equality, and the potential for gender inclusivity in the future of the sport.

Before we begin:

As is the case with a great number of other sports, cricket has traditionally been linked with ideas of masculinity and male superiority. Women's cricket, as well as attempts to challenge gender stereotypes and promote diversity, have been able to originate and flourish despite the sport's long-standing preference for the participation of men. This is because the sport does not discriminate on the basis of sexual orientation. In order to have a complete understanding of the intricate relationship that exists between cricket and gender dynamics, it is necessary to do an in-depth investigation of the sport's historical origins, the development of women's participation in cricket, the problems that female cricketers confront, and the initiatives that are designed to promote gender equality within the sport.

Cricket's Role in History as a Traditionally Masculine Activity

The historical setting of cricket reveals the sport's association with traditional gender roles as well as the notion of masculinity. The sport had its beginnings in England, and at first, only men participated in it and helped spread its popularity; women had little opportunity to join in at that time. There was very limited opportunity for women to participate actively in cricket during this time period due to the cultural and societal standards that perpetuated the idea that cricket was a male activity.

As cricket became more popular and moved to other regions, particularly the British colonies, its long-standing link with masculine superiority and power became more ingrained.

This historical bias contributed to the marginalization of women in the cricketing arena, which in turn contributed to the continuation of gender imbalances and limited chances for female participation in the sport.

The Development of Cricket for Women

In spite of the fact that cricket has traditionally been associated with masculinity, the landscape of women's cricket has seen a considerable shift over the course of the last several decades. The acknowledgment and development of women's cricket have led to a sea change in the gender dynamics that exist within the sport. As a result, new chances and platforms have been created for female cricketers to demonstrate their aptitude and skills.

On the global scale, the introduction of women's cricket leagues and tournaments, such as the Women's Cricket World Cup and numerous Twenty20 contests, has been an essential factor in increasing the visibility of female cricketers and the acclaim they receive for their accomplishments. Not only have these initiatives improved the standing of women's cricket, but they have also challenged prejudices and perceptions regarding women's participation in sports that are usually thought to be male-dominated.

Obstacles that Female Cricket Players Must Overcome

In spite of the strides that have been achieved to advance women's cricket, female cricket players still have to contend with a wide range of difficulties and roadblocks that impede their ability to participate and advance in the sport. There has been a continuing problem with the gender gap when it comes to salary, resources, facilities, and media coverage. This problem is reflective of larger systemic inequalities that exist within the cricketing globe.

The pay difference that exists between male and female cricketers has been a particularly sensitive subject, bringing attention to the fact that there is already a gender salary discrepancy within the sport of cricket. Despite having equivalent skills and making comparable contributions to the sport of cricket, female cricketers typically earn a substantially lower salary than their male counterparts. This difference not only diminishes the importance of women's cricket but also contributes to the broader devaluation of women's athletics.

Significant difficulties have also been caused by the lack of suitable facilities, training opportunities, and resources for female cricket players, which has restricted their access to professional coaching, infrastructure, and support systems. The lack of investment in women's cricket has hampered the development of talent as well as the overall expansion of the sport. This has resulted in obstacles being placed in the path of ambitious female cricketers, making it more difficult for them to thrive and compete at the top levels.

A further factor that has contributed to the underrepresentation of female cricket players in the public realm is the low media coverage and visibility of women's cricket. There has been a negative impact on the general promotion and popularization of women's cricket as a result of the lack of exposure and recognition in mainstream media. As a result, it is difficult for female players to achieve recognition and establish a loyal fan base.

Efforts Made Towards Achieving Gender Parity In Cricket

In response to the necessity of addressing gender discrepancies within the sport, a number of initiatives and programs that promote gender equality and inclusivity have been put into place. These programs have focused on tackling the systemic challenges that female cricketers encounter, pushing for equitable opportunities and resources, and cultivating an environment that is more welcoming and encouraging for women who participate in cricket.

The adoption of gender-inclusive policies and activities by cricket's governing bodies and other organizations is a noteworthy initiative that deserves recognition. The International Cricket Council (ICC) and national cricket boards have both taken aggressive steps to promote gender equality and to create a playing field that is more equitable for male and female cricket players. These steps were taken in order to make the sport more inclusive. These initiatives have included things like the formation of women's cricket committees, the provision of resources for the advancement of women's cricket, and the incorporation of gender-sensitive policies into the governing structures of cricket.

In addition, the establishment of women's cricket leagues and tournaments on both the domestic and international levels has given female cricket players a stage on which to demonstrate their abilities and compete at a level appropriate for a professional sport. These leagues have not only increased the visibility of women's cricket, but they have also encouraged the participation of young girls and aspiring cricketers. As a result, they have helped to cultivate a culture within the sport that is inclusive of women and empowers them.

Education and awareness programs that promote gender equality and challenge gender stereotypes have also played an important role in the transformation of the landscape of cricket. This has been one of the most significant contributors to the change. These programs have endeavored to educate players, coaches, administrators, and spectators on the significance of gender inclusivity and the benefits of women's participation in the sport of cricket. These activities have helped to the creation of an environment that is more supportive of female cricketers by questioning old conventions and perceptions. [T]hey did this by challenging traditional norms and preconceptions.

The Prospects for Equal Participation of Men and Women in Cricket

As cricket continues to embrace diversity and equality among its participants, the future of gender inclusiveness in the sport holds a great deal of promise. A positive change toward a more equitable and inclusive cricketing landscape is indicated by the increased recognition and support for women's cricket as well as the introduction of gender-inclusive policies and programs. Together, these developments point to a shift in the right direction.

It will be essential to continue promoting women's cricket leagues, tournaments, and grassroots development initiatives in order to nurture and cultivate the talent of prospective female cricket players. The governing bodies of cricket have the ability to empower the next generation of female cricketers and pave the road for their success and progress within the sport if they provide equal chances, resources, and support.

The existing gaps can be closed and a fair playing field created for both male and female players with the help of investments in infrastructure, training facilities, and coaching programs that are designed for female cricketers. Cricketing authorities may build a more inclusive and diverse sporting culture by promoting the growth of women's cricket at all levels. This can, in turn, foster a sense of belonging and empowerment among female cricketers.

It will also be vital, in order to drive long-term structural change, to promote gender inclusiveness in leadership roles and decision-making positions within cricket governing bodies. Cricketing companies can establish a more equitable and progressive environment for all stakeholders if they promote a culture of diversity and inclusion as well as a larger representation of women in leadership roles and encourage more women to run for leadership positions.

Additionally, continuing advocacy and awareness initiatives that are focused on breaking gender stereotypes and promoting gender equality in cricket will be extremely helpful in the process of cultivating a culture of respect and inclusivity within the sport. Cricket has the potential to serve as a catalyst for social change and empowerment by encouraging fans, media, and other stakeholders to participate in talks regarding gender dynamics and by supporting positive role models. These actions will hopefully encourage future generations to embrace diversity and equality in all facets of life.

The impact that cricket has had on gender dynamics has undergone tremendous change throughout the course of its history, with the sport moving away from its traditional status as a male-dominated area and toward a more welcoming and diverse atmosphere. Even though problems and inequalities still exist, there has been a good trend toward more gender equality in cricket, which can be seen in the increased recognition and support for women's cricket as well as the introduction of gender-inclusive policies and programs.

The process of achieving gender inclusion in cricket is an ongoing one, and various projects are currently under way to alleviate inequalities, promote equal opportunities, and challenge established conventions and prejudices. The sport of cricket continues to embrace diversity, empowering female cricketers, and inspiring future generations to appreciate the significance of equality and inclusivity in all facets of life. As a result, the future of gender inclusivity in the sport holds enormous promise.

Cricket has the potential to be a tremendous force for social change, encouraging a culture of respect, diversity, and empowerment both on and off the field of play. This is because of the sport's egalitarian and inclusive nature. As the game develops further, it has the potential to become a symbol of forward movement and an illustration of how gender inclusion can be achieved inside historically male-dominated sectors. This can serve as both an inspiration and a glimmer of hope for a world that is more equitable and welcoming to all people.

5.1 Women's cricket and its growth

Women's cricket, which was once dominated by its male counterpart, has witnessed substantial growth and recognition in recent years, receiving increasing support, visibility, and respect on the global arena. In the past, men's cricket was the dominant form of the sport. In the course of this 1000-word essay, I will present an in-depth examination of the expansion of women's cricket, covering its historical evolution, milestones accomplished, problems faced, and the future trajectory of the sport. I will begin by describing the current state of the sport.

Before we begin:

Women's cricket, which for a long time was ignored and ostracized, has recently emerged as a dynamic and fast rising sector of the sport, with a strong emphasis on fostering gender equality and inclusivity. The progression of women's cricket is reflective of a path that has been characterized by drive, resilience, and a dogged pursuit of recognition and acceptance. In order to have an understanding of the growth trajectory of women's cricket, it is necessary to investigate the historical context of the sport, the milestones that have been accomplished in the most recent years, the difficulties that are experienced by female cricket players, and the bright future that is in store for the sport.

The Development of Women's Cricket Throughout History

Women's cricket may be traced back to the late 18th century, with the earliest known women's cricket match taking place in England in 1745. The history of women's cricket can be traced back to the late 18th century. However, due to societal conventions and gender biases, women's involvement in organized sports was prohibited for a number of years, therefore their participation in cricket remained mostly informal and to a lesser extent than that of men.

It was not until the latter half of the 19th century and the early part of the 20th century that women's cricket started to achieve attention and importance, particularly in the countries of England and Australia. The establishment of women's cricket clubs and teams gave a stage upon which female cricketers could demonstrate their talents and dedication to the game, so setting the groundwork for the systematic growth of women's cricket in the decades to come.

Women's Cricket Has Reached a Number of Important Milestones

The development of women's cricket has been accompanied by a number of note-worthy milestones and accomplishments, all of which have contributed to the game's ascent to hitherto unattained levels of popularity and acknowledgement. The formation of the Women's Cricket Association (WCA) in England in 1926 was a watershed event in the annals of women's cricket. This event was significant because it established a formal organization that would be used for the development and administration of the sport.

In 1973, England played home to the first-ever Women's Cricket World Cup. This event was another watershed moment that brought women's cricket to the notice of the international community and helped pave the way for the sport's eventual expansion around the world. The competition highlighted the potential and skill of female cricketers from a variety of countries and helped pave the way for the founding of the International Women's Cricket Council (IWCC), the forerunner of the women's cricket section of the International Cricket Council (ICC).

As a result of the widespread acknowledgment that women's cricket is an essential component of the game of cricket around the world, the sport has been incorporated into multi-nation competitions such as the Commonwealth Games and the Asian Games. This has further solidified cricket's position as a mainstream athletic discipline.

Obstacles that Female Cricket Players Must Overcome

In spite of the expansion and increased awareness of women's cricket, female cricket players still have to deal with a variety of difficulties and roadblocks, which slows down their overall progression and development within the sport. There has been a continuing problem with the gender gap when it comes to salary, resources, facilities, and media coverage. This problem is reflective of larger systemic inequalities that exist within the cricketing globe.

Despite having identical abilities and accomplishments to the sport, female cricket-ers earn a
significantly lower salary than their male counterparts. This is despite the fact that the gender pay gap is still a big topic. The gap in remuneration not only highlights the undervaluation of women's cricket but also continues to perpetuate the devaluation of women's sports in general, underlining the requirement for more equity and respect for female athletes.

Inadequate resources, training facilities, and infrastructure for women's cricket have also caused obstacles, which has limited the access of female cricketers to possibilities for professional coaching and advancement in their careers. The lack of investments in women's cricket has impeded the growth of the sport and created difficulties for prospective female cricketers who want to succeed and compete at the top levels. Despite these obstacles, women's cricket continues to expand.

A further factor that has contributed to the underrepresentation of female cricket players in the public realm is the low media coverage and visibility of women's cricket. There has been a negative impact on the general promotion and popularization of women's cricket as a result of the lack of exposure and recognition in mainstream media. As a result, it is difficult for female players to achieve recognition and establish a loyal fan base.

Positive Prospects and a Stable Path to Development

In spite of the obstacles, it seems like women's cricket has a bright future ahead of it, especially because there is an increasing focus within the sport on encouraging gender inclusion, female empowerment, and equality. A good trend toward better equity and chances for female cricket players can be seen in the growing recognition and support for women's cricket, as well as the introduction of gender-inclusive policies and programs. These developments point to a change in the right direction.

It is essential to make investments in infrastructure, training facilities, and coaching programs that are specifically designed for female cricketers in order to close current disparities and create a level playing field for male and female players alike in cricket. The governing bodies of cricket have the ability to empower future generations of female cricketers and pave the path for the success and expansion of those players within the sport if they give top priority to the development of women's cricket at all levels.

Women's cricket needs more leagues, tournaments, and grassroots development programs if it wants to cultivate the potential of ambitious female cricketers and build a culture of inclusivity and empowerment within the sport. Promotion of women's cricket leagues, tournaments, and grassroots development programs will be crucial in achieving these goals. The authorities in charge of cricket can pave the way for women's cricket's continued expansion and success on the international arena by ensuring that all players have access to the same opportunities, resources, and support.

In addition, advocacy initiatives that target breaking gender stereotypes, supporting gender equality, and raising knowledge about the significance of women's participation in cricket will be vital in order to cultivate an environment that is more friendly and welcoming for female cricket players.

Cricket has the potential to serve as a catalyst for social change and empowerment if fans, the media, and other stakeholders are engaged in talks about the gender dynamics of the game and the significance of gender inclusion. This will inspire future generations to embrace diversity and equality in all facets of life.

A journey marked by dedication, endurance, and the unrelenting pursuit of recognition and respect can be seen reflected in the growth of women's cricket. Women's cricket has gone a long way in terms of defying gender stereotypes and fostering inclusivity and equality within the sport since its beginnings as a very minor subset of the larger sport of cricket. It is now considered a mainstream athletic discipline.

Both the achievements that have been made and the difficulties that have been encountered by female cricketers highlight the necessity of continuing efforts to create a more fair and supportive environment for women who participate in cricket. Cricketing authorities can pave the way for the sustained growth and success of women's cricket by addressing gender disparities, promoting gender-inclusive policies, and investing in the development of women's cricket. This will inspire future generations to embrace diversity and equality in all facets of life.

5.2 Gender dynamics within cricket

Cricket, like many other sports, has traditionally been dominated by men and is characterized by gender inequities. Women have been underrepresented in the sport. However, in recent years there has been a substantial movement in the gender dynamics within the sport, with a greater emphasis on encouraging gender inclusivity and equality. This shift has occurred alongside a growing awareness of the importance of gender equality. This essay of 1000 words will provide a complete examination of the gender dynamics within cricket. It will investigate the historical setting of the sport, the changing position of women, the obstacles experienced by female cricketers, initiatives for gender equality, and the potential for gender inclusivity in the sport in the future.

Before we begin:

Cricket, which is generally considered to be a male-dominated activity, has recently witnessed a transition in its gender dynamics. This change has been brought about by a desire for inclusivity and gender equality. There has been a long tradition of male participation and leadership in the sport of cricket; nevertheless, there is now a rising awareness of the role that women play in the sport. In order to have an understanding of the shifting gender dynamics within cricket, it is necessary to investigate the historical backdrop of the sport, the shifting roles of women, the difficulties encountered by female cricketers, initiatives designed to create gender equality, and the future trajectory of gender inclusivity.

Cricket was traditionally a male-dominated sport throughout its entire history

The historical setting of cricket reveals the sport's association with traditional gender roles as well as the notion of masculinity. The sport had its beginnings in England, and at first, only men participated in it and helped spread its popularity; women had little opportunity to join in at that time. There was limited opportunity for women to take part in organized cricket at the time since societal conventions and gender prejudices of the period reinforced the impression that cricket was predominantly a male hobby. As a result, the sport was dominated by men.

During the 19th and early 20th centuries, the cultural and social standards of those time periods contributed to the marginalization of women in the sport of cricket. These norms indicated that it was unacceptable for women to participate in sports such as cricket, often due to concerns about the amount of physical exertion involved and the potential for the activity to upset established gender roles. As a direct consequence of this, the participation of women in cricket has remained primarily informal and restricted, with little opportunity for organized competition or access to formal instruction.

Women's Cricket and Their Changing Roles in the Sport

In spite of the fact that men have historically held a participation advantage in cricket, women's cricket has made great progress in recent decades. The acknowledgment and promotion of women's cricket have led to a revolution in the gender dynamics within the sport, leading to the creation of new possibilities and platforms for female cricketers to showcase their talent and talents. This has led to a transformation in the gender dynamics within the sport.

The establishment of women's cricket clubs and teams in the latter half of the 19th century set the groundwork for the growth of organized women's cricket in the next century. These early pioneers defied society standards and gender biases, thereby paving the way for women to take an active role in the sport they were participating in.

The formation of the Women's Cricket Association (WCA) in England in 1926 was a watershed event in the annals of women's cricket. This event was significant because it established a formal organization that would be used for the development and administration of the sport. This was the beginning of organized women's cricket at the international level, and the following year, in 1973, England played home to the first Women's Cricket World Cup.

As a result of women's cricket being included in multi-national competitions like the Commonwealth Games and the Asian Games, the role of women in the sport has been further reinforced, and hurdles and misconceptions around their involvement have been broken down.

Obstacles that Female Cricket Players Must Overcome

In spite of the strides that have been achieved to advance women's cricket, female cricket players still have to contend with a wide range of difficulties and roadblocks that impede their ability to participate and advance in the sport. There is still a gender gap in terms of salary, resources, facilities, and media coverage, which is reflective of greater systemic inequalities within the world of cricket.

Even if they have equivalent talents and accomplishments to the sport, female cricketers get a significantly lower salary than their male counterparts. This is despite the fact that the gender pay gap continues to be a big issue. The gap in remuneration not only highlights the undervaluation of women's cricket but also continues to perpetuate the devaluation of women's sports in general, underlining the requirement for more equity and respect for female athletes.

The lack of proper funding, training facilities, and infrastructure for women's cricket has also posed significant problems. As a result, the options for professional coaching and development that are available to female cricket players have been restricted. Because there has been a dearth of investment in women's cricket, the growth of the sport has been stunted, which has made it more difficult for aspiring female cricket players to excel and compete at the highest levels.

Due in part to the lack of media coverage and visibility accorded to women's cricket, female cricket players are underrepresented in the public realm. There has been a negative impact on the general promotion and popularization of women's cricket as a result of the lack of exposure and recognition in mainstream media. As a result, it is difficult for female players to achieve recognition and establish a loyal fan base.

Efforts Made Towards Achieving Gender Parity In Cricket

In response to the necessity of addressing gender discrepancies within the sport, a number of initiatives and programs that promote gender equality and inclusivity have been put into place. These programs have focused on tackling the systemic challenges that female cricketers encounter, pushing for equitable opportunities and resources, and cultivating an environment that is more welcoming and encouraging for women who participate in cricket.

The adoption of policies and initiatives that welcome players of both sexes by cricket's governing bodies and other organizations is an important step that has been taken. The International Cricket Council (ICC) and national cricket boards have both taken aggressive steps to promote gender equality and to create a playing field that is more equitable for male and female cricket players. These steps were taken in order to make the sport more inclusive.

Among these initiatives are the formation of women's cricket committees, the provision of resources for the advancement of women's cricket, and the incorporation of gender-sensitive policies into the governance structures of cricket.

As a result of the establishment of women's cricket leagues and tournaments on both the domestic and international levels, female cricket players now have the opportunity to demonstrate their abilities and compete at a level appropriate for a professional sport. These leagues have not only increased the visibility of women's cricket, but they have also encouraged the participation of young girls and aspiring cricketers. As a result, they have helped to cultivate a culture within the sport that is inclusive of women and empowers them.

Education and awareness programs that promote gender equality and challenge gender stereotypes have also played an important role in the transformation of the landscape of cricket. This has been one of the most significant contributors to the change. These programs have endeavored to educate players, coaches, administrators, and spectators on the significance of gender inclusivity and the benefits of women's participation in the sport of cricket. These activities have helped to the creation of an environment that is more supportive of female cricketers by questioning old conventions and perceptions. [T]hey did this by challenging traditional norms and preconceptions.

The Prospects for Equal Participation of Men and Women in Cricket

As cricket continues to embrace diversity and equality among its participants, the future of gender inclusiveness in the sport holds a great deal of promise. An encouraging step in the right direction toward more gender equality within the sport is being taken, and it can be seen in the growing recognition and support for women's cricket as well as the introduction of policies and programs that are gender-inclusive.

It will be essential to make investments in infrastructure, training facilities, and coaching programs designed specifically for female cricketers in order to close the existing disparities and create a level playing field for male and female players alike in cricket. The governing bodies of cricket have the ability to inspire the next generation of female cricketers and pave the road for their future achievements and advancements within the sport if they make the development of women's cricket a priority at all levels.

The skill of ambitious female cricketers may be nurtured to its full potential through the expansion of women's cricket leagues, tournaments, and grassroots development programs. The governing bodies of cricket have the ability to inspire young females and aspiring cricket players to achieve their goals by cultivating a culture of empowerment and inclusivity within the sport. This may be accomplished by offering equal chances, resources, and support.

It will also be vital, in order to drive long-term structural change, to promote gender inclusiveness in leadership roles and decision-making positions within cricket governing bodies. Cricketing companies can establish a more equitable and progressive environment for all stakeholders if they promote a culture of diversity and inclusion as well as a larger representation of women in leadership roles and encourage more women to run for leadership positions.

Additionally, continuing advocacy and awareness initiatives that are focused on breaking gender stereotypes and promoting gender equality in cricket will be extremely helpful in the process of cultivating a culture of respect and inclusivity within the sport. Cricket has the potential to serve as a catalyst for social change and empowerment by encouraging fans, media, and other stakeholders to participate in talks regarding gender dynamics and by supporting positive role models. These actions will hopefully encourage future generations to embrace diversity and equality in all facets of life.

Cricket has transitioned from a historically male-dominated sport into a more inclusive and diverse environment, with a rising emphasis on encouraging gender equality and inclusivity. This change came about as a result of an increase in the number of female players in the sport. Both the achievements that have been made and the difficulties that have been encountered by female cricketers highlight the necessity of continuing efforts to create a more fair and

supportive environment for women who participate in cricket.

The process of achieving gender inclusion in cricket is an ongoing one, and various projects are currently under way to alleviate inequalities, promote equal opportunities, and challenge established conventions and prejudices. The sport of cricket continues to embrace diversity, empowering female cricketers, and inspiring future generations to appreciate the significance of equality and inclusivity in all facets of life. As a result, the future of gender inclusivity in the sport holds enormous promise.

Cricket has the potential to be a tremendous force for social change, encouraging a culture of respect, diversity, and empowerment both on and off the field of play. This is because of the sport's egalitarian and inclusive nature. As the sport continues to develop, it has the potential to serve as an example of how gender inclusion can be achieved within traditionally male-dominated arenas. This can serve as both an inspiration and a glimmer of hope for a world that is more equal and inclusive.

5.3 The changing landscape of women's participation in the sport

The landscape of women's participation in athletics has experienced a profound transition over the past few decades, highlighted by considerable achievements in gender inclusivity, acknowledgment, and empowerment. This transformation has been marked by significant advancements in gender equality. This essay of 1000 words will provide a comprehensive analysis of the changing landscape of women's participation in sports, with a specific focus on the evolving role of women in various sporting disciplines, the challenges they have faced, the milestones achieved, and the future trajectory of gender inclusivity in sports. Specifically, this focus will be on the evolving role of women in various sporting disciplines, the challenges they have faced, the milestones achieved, and the future trajectory of gender inclusivity in sports.

Before we begin:

There has been a tremendous transformation in the views and conventions of society, which has led to more recognition and possibilities for female athletes. This movement is reflected in the shifting landscape of women's engagement in sports. In spite of the fact that women have traditionally been subjected to a plethora of obstacles and difficulties in the sporting world, there has been a discernible shift in the perception and acceptance of women's participation in a variety of sporting activities in recent years. Exploring the historical context, the challenges faced by female athletes, the milestones achieved in promoting gender inclusivity, and the future prospects for fostering a more equitable and empowering sporting environment are necessary in order to gain an understanding of the shifting landscape of women's participation in sports.

The Obstacles and Obstacle-Climbing Experiences of Women Athletes Throughout History

The historical context of women's participation in sports has been marked by widespread gender stereotypes, cultural biases, and structural impediments that have limited their access to opportunities to participate in sporting activities. The traditional gender norms typically dictated that it was undesirable or even frowned upon for women to participate in sports, which resulted in a lack of support and resources for female athletes.

In the early 20th century, women's participation in sports began to emerge, albeit in restricted capacities and subject to stringent societal restraints. This trend continued throughout the century. The development of women's sports groups and contests gave a stage upon which female athletes could exhibit their skills; yet, they frequently encountered opposition and discrimination from mainstream sporting institutions.

The marginalization of female athletes was further contributed to by the lack of money, resources, and media attention for women's sports. This helped to perpetuate the idea that sports were primarily a male domain. As a direct consequence of this, the participation of women in sports has continued to be generally ignored and underestimated, which restricts the options available to them for recognition and success in the world of sports.

The Changing Place of Women in Competitive Sports

Female athletes have shown that they are resilient and determined to overcome hurdles and

carve out a position for themselves in the sporting arena, as has been proved by the evolving role of women in sports despite the challenges that have been presented to them historically. Traditional gender norms and prejudices have been challenged as a result of the growing visibility and representation of women in a variety of sports, including soccer, basketball, tennis, and athletics. As a result, the narrative of women's participation in sports has been rewritten to reflect these challenges.

Beginning in the early 20th century, the inclusion of women athletes in the Olympic Games was a key step forward in the movement toward greater gender equality in athletics. This achievement was acknowledged by the passage of a milestone. To assist enhance the status of women's sports and provide a global platform for female athletes to compete at the highest levels, new athletic disciplines and events that are geared specifically for female athletes have been incorporated into the sport scene.

The advent of notable female athletes such as Billie Jean King, Serena Williams, and Marta Vieira da Silva, amongst others, has further contributed to the recognition and celebration of women's achievements in sports. Specifically, this has been the case with tennis players Billie Jean King, Serena Williams, and Marta Vieira da Silva. These trailblazing athletes have inspired generations of women to pursue their sporting aspirations and have become advocates for gender equality and diversity in sports. Their accomplishments have paved the way for other women to follow in their footsteps.

Obstacles That Female Athletes Must Overcome

Female athletes continue to encounter a variety of hurdles and obstacles that impede their participation and advancement within the sporting world, despite the progress that has been achieved to promote gender inclusivity in sports. Despite these advances, female athletes continue to confront these challenges and obstacles. There is still a continuing problem with gender inequality in terms of salary, resources, facilities, and media coverage. This problem is reflective of deeper systemic inequalities that exist within the sports sector.

There is still a huge problem with the pay gap between men and women, which results in female athletes frequently earning less than their male counterparts, while having comparable skills and achievements. The gap in compensation not only lowers the value of the sports that women participate in, but it also ensures that the contributions that female athletes make to the sporting world will never be properly recognized or appreciated.

Significant obstacles have been presented by the lack of proper resources, training facilities, and support systems for female athletes. This has resulted in a restriction of the options available to female athletes for professional coaching and growth. As a result of insufficient funding for women's sports, the growth and development of female athletes has been hampered, which has made it more difficult for young women with aspirations of excelling and competing at the top levels.

The underrepresentation of female athletes in the public sphere has been further contributed to by the restricted media coverage and visibility of women's sports. It is difficult for female athletes to achieve fame and develop a loyal fan base as a result of the lack of exposure and recognition that women's sports receive in mainstream media, which has a negative impact on the overall promotion and popularization of women's sports.

Progress Made Towards Fostering an Environment That Is Inclusive of All Genders

In the most recent years, major advances have been made in the promotion of gender equality and empowerment in the realm of athletics. In order to combat the structural obstacles that female athletes must overcome and to promote equality in terms of chances and resources within the sporting world, a number of different initiatives and programs have been put into place.

The implementation of gender-inclusive policies and programs by sports governing bodies and organizations has played a significant part in the advancement of gender equality and the creation of a more level playing field for male and female athletes. This has been one of the most important factors in the success of these endeavors. These initiatives have included the implementation of measures for pay parity, the allocation of resources for the growth of women's sports, and the incorporation of gender-sensitive policies into the governing structures of sports organizations.

Female athletes now have the opportunity to demonstrate their skills and compete at a professional level thanks to the establishment of women's sports leagues and tournaments on both the national and international levels. These programs have not only increased the awareness of women's sports, but they have also encouraged the participation of young girls and aspiring athletes. As a result, they have helped to develop a culture of inclusivity and empowerment within the world of sports.

Education and awareness initiatives centered on promoting gender equality and challenging gender stereotypes have also played a significant role in the transformation of the sports scene. This has been one of the most important factors in the overall success of the movement.

These initiatives have sought to educate athletes, coaches, administrators, and spectators on the significance of gender inclusivity and the value of women's participation in sports in the hopes of creating an environment that is more supportive and welcoming for female athletes.

The Prospects for Egalitarianism in Competitive Sports

As the sports business continues to embrace diversity, equality, and empowerment, there is reason to be optimistic about the future of gender inclusiveness in the sporting world. In order to close the inequalities that currently exist and provide a level playing field for male and female participants, it will be essential to make investments in infrastructure, training facilities, and coaching programs that are specifically designed for female athletes.

The cultivation of the skills of future female athletes will be greatly aided by the expansion of women's sports leagues, tournaments, and grassroots development programs. The governing bodies of sports have the ability to empower the next generation of female athletes and prepare the path for the success and growth of these athletes within the world of sports if they provide equal chances, resources, and support.

It will be vital to continue lobbying and awareness initiatives that are focused on overcoming gender stereotypes and promoting gender equality in athletics if the sports business is ever going to cultivate a culture of respect and inclusivity for its members. Sports have the potential to serve as a catalyst for social change and empowerment. This can be accomplished by engaging fans, the media, and other stakeholders in talks about gender dynamics and by supporting positive role models. This will inspire future generations to embrace diversity and equality in all facets of life.

The landscape of women's engagement in sports is shifting, which represents a significant transformation in the views and conventions of society. This movement has resulted in increased recognition and opportunities for female athletes. Even though many obstacles still need to be overcome, the strides that have been made toward increasing gender equality and female empowerment in sports represent a step in the right direction toward greater parity and opportunity for female athletes.

The process of achieving gender inclusion in sports is an ongoing one, with projects currently underway to redress inequalities, promote equal opportunities, and challenge established conventions and prejudices. As long as the sports business continues to celebrate diversity, encourages female athletes to compete at their highest level, and encourages future generations to realize the value of equality and inclusivity in all facets of life, there is reason to be optimistic about the future of gender inclusivity in sports.

Both on and off the field, athletic competition has the ability to serve as a formidable agent of social transformation by fostering an environment that values variety, respect, and empowerment. As the sector continues to develop, it has the potential to demonstrate how gender inclusion can be achieved inside historically male-dominated settings, so serving as a source of motivation and hope for the creation of a more equal and inclusive world.

Chapter 6

Cricket and Development

Cricket, which is frequently praised for being more than just a sport, has been a significant contributor to development programs all around the world. The sport's effect extends much beyond the confines of the playing field and may be seen in various aspects of societal, economic, and individual advancement. This article, which is 3000 words long, dives into the complex relationship that exists between cricket and development. Specifically, it investigates the ways in which the sport has contributed to the development of communities, economies, and individuals.

Before we begin:

The sport of cricket, which was formerly thought of as a colonial inheritance, has developed into a global phenomenon with far-reaching ramifications. The sport has unquestionably provided a source of entertainment for millions of people, but it has also been utilized as a vehicle for growth, contributing to the advancement of society, the economy, and individuals in a variety of settings. This article presents a comprehensive investigation into the complex relationship that exists between cricket and development. The author investigates the role that the sport plays in the formation of communities, the expansion of economies, and the progress of individuals.

Cricket and the Development of Community

Cricket has been shown to be an effective agent in the process of community building. It does

this by promoting a sense of belonging and unity among those who take part in and watch the game. The power of the sport to bring people together transcends both geographical and cultural borders. It provides a common ground on which individuals can connect with one another, rejoice together, and work together.

Cricket Associations and Clubs in Your Neighborhood:

Cricket associations and clubs in the surrounding area function as centers of community participation. They serve as a gathering spot for individuals from a variety of walks of life, which helps to cultivate friendships and a sense of community. These clubs frequently arrange youth programs, community events, and humanitarian activities, all of which contribute to the strengthening of the communities' social fabric.

The Power of Cricket to Bring People Together:

Cricket is more than just a sport in many nations, including India, Pakistan, the West Indies, and England; it is also a unifying force that brings together people from many different ethnicities. Cricket matches have the ability to establish a sense of shared identity and pride among spectators, regardless of the spectators' language, religion, or social level.

Development at the Grassroots:

Young children are introduced to the sport of cricket through grassroots programs, which give these children a constructive and welcoming pastime to participate in with their peers. Not only do these programs teach cricket skills, but they also teach life lessons such as the need for collaboration, discipline, and sportsmanship.

The Role of Global Events as Unifying Platforms:

The International Cricket Council (ICC) Cricket World Cup, the International Cricket Council

Twenty20 World Cup, and bilateral series between countries all draw millions of spectators worldwide. These events frequently foster cultural dialogue and diplomatic relations, contributing to the construction of bridges between nations.

Cricket and the Expansion of the Economy

Cricket has turned into a lucrative sector that has made important contributions to the economic expansion of both industrialized nations and emerging nations. The financial potential of the sport has opened up doors for the development of tourism and infrastructure as well as for the creation of new jobs.

Creating New Jobs:

Employment opportunities are available in the cricket industry for a diverse spectrum of professionals, such as cricketers, coaches, umpires, ground workers, marketing gurus, and event organizers. In addition, the sport is responsible for the maintenance of a huge economic ecology that includes everything from broadcasters to manufacturers of sporting goods.

Tourism:

Many visitors from different parts of the world attend major cricketing events. The hosting of these events can be beneficial to the local economy because it will likely result in an increase in visitors, hotel bookings, and spending during match days.

The Development of Infrastructure:

The construction of cricket stadiums and other facilities requires large investments, which ultimately results in the improvement of urban development and infrastructure.

These facilities also have the capability of serving as multi-purpose venues for a variety of events, which can contribute to the overall economic growth of regions.

Potential Profits from Business:

Sponsorships, merchandise sales, and the sale of media rights all contribute significantly to the cash that cricket franchises and boards bring in. The sport's commercial appeal has resulted in the formation of a large number of brand collaborations, which has further contributed to the sport's economic impact.

The Game of Cricket and Its Effect on Personal Growth

The activity of cricket has the ability to propel an individual's personal development by teaching them vital life skills, encouraging the formation of their character, and providing a route to achieving their own sense of fulfillment.

Developing One's Capabilities:

Cricket is a sport that needs a variety of talents, including physical, mental, and technical. Not only does honing and perfecting these abilities boost cricket performance, but they also strengthen an individual's capacity to concentrate, devise new strategies, and adjust to changing circumstances.

Respect for Oneself and One's Work:

Cricket is a sport that requires a high level of discipline and a solid work ethic. These principles are applicable to a variety of facets of life, including the pursuit of an education and a profession, for example.

Leadership and Collaborative Efforts:

Cricket is a sport that gives individuals the opportunity to participate in team leadership roles and work together with others in a collaborative setting. Through participation in these activities, participants develop leadership and teamwork skills that are useful in a variety of settings.

Capacity for Bouncing Back and Emotional Intelligence:

Cricket is a sport that can be mentally taxing due to its unpredictable nature, which includes highs and lows, failures and victories. Players have the ability to handle pressure, become more resilient, and enhance their emotional intelligence as a result of their participation in the game, all of which can benefit them in their personal and professional lives.

Inspirations & People to Look Up To:

Cricketers who achieve success frequently go on to serve as models for younger athletes. They encourage young people to dream large, to create objectives for themselves, and to work very hard to accomplish those goals.

Initiatives in Cricket for International Development

Cricket for development initiatives are programs and projects that use the sport to address societal and economic issues. These issues can be addressed through the use of cricket. These efforts typically have the goal of bringing about positive change in a number of different elements of one's life.

Instructional Methods Utilizing Cricket:

Cricket is being used in a variety of educational outreach projects all around the world. Children from disadvantaged backgrounds might have access to educational opportunities thanks to these programs, which gives them a chance to enhance their chances for the future.

Cricket's Contribution to the Emancipation of Women

In recent years, women's cricket has been gaining popularity, which has helped to empower women and break down gender barriers. It is possible for gender equality to be advanced by societal changes brought about by initiatives aimed at increasing the number of women who participate in sporting events.

Initiatives Regarding Health and Wellness:

The health and fitness of players can be improved through the sport of cricket. Lifestyles that are healthier and more physically active are associated with the benefits of programs that encourage active engagement in sports.

The development of communities:

The use of cricket as a tool to improve communities as a whole is the primary emphasis of community improvement initiatives that are centered on the sport of cricket. These projects may include the building of infrastructure, the training of individuals in vocational fields, and support for populations who are disadvantaged.

Restoring Harmony and Compatibility:

In areas that have been afflicted by conflict, the sport of cricket has been utilized as a tool for peacebuilding and reconciliation. Competitions in a variety of sports have the potential to bridge the gaps in communication and cooperation that exist between communities, regardless of political or ethnic affiliation.

The Obstacles and the Criticisms

Disparities in Obtaining Access:

In many areas, getting a chance to play cricket, especially at a high enough level to be competitive, might be difficult. Disadvantaged persons, particularly those from lower socioeconomic backgrounds, may not be able to derive the full benefits of participating in sports.

The Process of Commoditization and Exploitation:

The commercialization of cricket, with its multi-million-dollar contracts and endorsements, might result in a concentration on profit rather than on the development outcomes that are being pursued. Because of the marketing of the game, gamers may be subjected to additional pressures and temptations.

Disparities Between the Sexes:

Even though women's cricket has made considerable strides forward, there are still major gender gaps in many regions of the world. Ongoing support is required for initiatives that seek to develop women's cricket and gender equality.

Long-term viability:

There may be difficulties in ensuring the long-term viability of cricket for development efforts. It may be difficult for certain programs to get long-term funding and support, which can have a negative impact on their capacity to bring about changes that are sustainable.

Cricket's contribution to development efforts is multi-faceted, with the sport acting as a catalyst for community building, economic growth, and individual development in addition to its role as a development tool. Cricket has the potential to bring people of different cultures together, to provide people the tools they need to make better lives for themselves, and to contribute to the economic growth of regions.

Although there are obstacles and criticisms, cricket for development efforts continue to have a substantial positive impact despite these factors. The sport's ability to motivate, alter, and bring about positive change in communities all over the world is illustrative of its everlasting relevance that extends beyond the confines of the playing field. In the next years, the role that cricket plays in development efforts is expected to grow even more significant and far-reaching as it continues to expand and adapt. This is because cricket is a sport that is played over a long period of time.

6.1 The economic impact of cricket

Cricket, which is frequently considered to be more than just a sport, has developed into a global industry that has huge repercussions for the economy. This essay of 1000 words dives into the multidimensional economic impact of cricket, analyzing how the sport generates income, stimulates job opportunities, promotes tourism, and drives commercial activities. The study examines how cricket generates revenue, stimulates job opportunities, boosts tourism, and drives commercial activities. In addition to this, it investigates the economic discrepancies that exist within the globe of cricket as well as the potential for the sport to contribute to economic growth in both developed and developing nations.

Before we begin:

Cricket is not only a sport that can excite the passions of millions of people all over the world, but it is also a big contribution to the economy on a global scale. The economic influence of cricket is felt far beyond the boundaries of the cricket stadium, and encompasses a variety of commercial activities, employment opportunities, and revenue-generating avenues. This article presents a comprehensive review of the economic impact of cricket, illuminating the importance of the sport to economies, employment, tourism, and commercial endeavors. In addition to this, it discusses the economic discrepancies that exist within the world of cricket as well as the potential for cricket to be a driver of economic development, particularly in poorer nations.

Producing Money or Revenue

Legal Rights to Broadcast:

The rights to broadcast cricket on television and internet platforms contribute significantly to the sport's overall earnings. Massive crowds are drawn to the most important cricketing events, such as the ICC Cricket World Cup and premier bilateral series, which results in lucrative deals being struck with media corporations. These contracts not only bring in money for the various cricket governing bodies, but they also bring in a large amount of money for the various broadcast networks.

Advertising and Sponsorship Opportunities:

Cricket has a massive fan base, which makes it an appealing medium for brands to associate themselves with and place their advertisements on. Companies on a worldwide and local scale invest extensively in cricket sponsorship and advertising partnerships as a means of connecting with the people they want to reach. This helps the sport's overall economic impact, as sponsorships are frequently a big part of the revenue that is brought in by cricket boards.

The sale of tickets and other merchandise:

Cricket grounds are packed with spectators who pay to see live matches, which results in

money from ticket sales. In addition, cricket gear, including as jerseys, souvenirs, and cricket equipment, is sold all over the world, providing a strong market for businesses that sell goods related to sports.

Competitions for Franchises:

The Indian Premier League (IPL), the Big Bash League (BBL), and the Pakistan Super League (PSL) are just a few examples of the franchise-based Twenty20 competitions that have become important cash producers. These leagues blend the excitement of sports competition with other forms of entertainment, which helps them draw in enormous crowds and bring in significant cash through franchise fees, ticket sales, and media rights.

Possibilities of Employment

The sport of cricket provides a diverse array of employment prospects in a variety of fields. The importance of the sport on the development of jobs is not restricted to professional cricket players; rather, it extends to coaches, support staff, event management professionals, sports journalists, ground workers, and a great number of other occupations.

Participants in Cricket and Support Staff:

At the heart of the sport of cricket are its professional players, as well as the coaches, physiotherapists, nutritionists, and analysts who work with them. They comprise a significant percentage of the labor in cricket, earning money and taking part in a variety of leagues and tournaments.

Staff on the Ground and Management of the Venue:

A vast number of people are employed in various capacities, including management and maintenance of cricket stadiums. The efficient running of matches and tournaments relies heavily on the efforts of groundsmen, other members of the security staff, and experts working in event administration.

In the world of media and broadcasting:

One of the most important contributors to the labor market is the media industry that surrounds cricket. This sector includes sports journalists, television crews, and commentators. Broadcasting cricket matches and providing coverage of the game requires a staff comprised of a wide range of individuals possessing a variety of abilities.

When it comes to marketing and branding:

Because of the breadth of its commercial activity, cricket requires the services of marketing and branding experts. This comprises those who are involved in the negotiations of sponsorships, the promotion of events, and the management of brands.

The retail industry and merchandise:

Jobs in the retail industry are generated by the sale of cricket items such as gear and equipment. The demand for cricket-related products is essential to the success of brick-and-mortar and online sporting goods retailers.

The Hospitality and Tourism Industry

Significant tourist and hospitality-related economic activity is driven in large part by cricket, notably the sport's main events and tours. The influx of cricket supporters, spectators, and tourists who attend cricket matches and events is beneficial to the economies of the countries and towns that play home to these competitions.

Tourism for Match Days:

The staging of cricket matches brings in tourists from both within the country and from beyond. Traveling to see the games in person generates cash for the tourism industry in the form of hotel reservations, meals at area restaurants, and participation in other local events.

Reservations at Hotels:

Major cricket tournaments frequently result in an increase in the number of hotel bookings and available rooms, which is beneficial to the hospitality industry. These events result in an increase in the demand for lodging, particularly in metropolitan areas that contain cricket stadiums.

Activities of a Cultural and Recreational Nature:

Cricket tours give visitors the chance to learn about the local history and see the sights of the country that is playing home to the event. Revenue from tourism is increased since many cricket fans mix attending matches with other activities like sightseeing and recreational pursuits.

Activities Related to Business

The economic impact of cricket is greatly bolstered by the various business endeavors that are intrinsically linked to the sport. Activities such as sponsorships, advertising, merchandise, and leagues based on franchises are included in this category.

Advertising and Sponsorship Opportunities:

Deals struck between cricket governing bodies, individual teams, and businesses for the purpose of sponsorship bring financial support to the game. Through these collaborations, advertisers are provided with opportunities to showcase their businesses during competitions like matches and tournaments.

Products for Sale and License Agreements:

The market for cricket memorabilia, such as jerseys, hats, and souvenirs, is a rich one for merchants who sell such items as well as the producers who sell them. Businesses are able to make officially licensed cricket products if they have a license to do so.

Competitions for Franchises:

Significant amounts of commercial activity are involved in franchise-based T20 leagues like the Indian Premier League and the Big Bash League. These leagues receive investments from franchise owners, corporate sponsors, and advertising, which drives economic activity associated to the ownership of teams and the marketing of brands.

Disparities in Economic Status Throughout the World of Cricket

In spite of the fact that cricket has a significant positive impact on the economy, there are significant economic inequalities within the cricketing world. Cricketing nations that are already prosperous typically reap the greatest benefits from the sport in terms of cash production, job prospects, and commercial activity. These differences can be linked to a number of different reasons, such as the level of popularity of the sport in a particular country, the size of the cricketing market, and the financial capability of cricket boards and franchises.

The Dominance of the Big Three:

The Board of Control for Cricket in India (BCCI), the England and Wales Cricket Board (ECB), and Cricket Australia (CA) are known as the "Big Three" cricket boards because of their major impact in international cricket. They have an economic advantage over other cricketing nations because of their financial clout, which enables them to negotiate lucrative television deals, attract sponsorships, and host tournaments that generate a lot of income for themselves.

The Twenty20 Leagues:

The tremendous popularity of Twenty20 competitions, most notably the Indian Premier League (IPL), has contributed significantly to India's growing economy. The revenue generation and commercial operations of the league have established a standard that is difficult for other countries that play cricket to compete with.

Calendar of Cricket Matches Played Around the World:

Richer nations typically have a larger control over the schedule that is used for international cricket, which enables them to organize matches and series that bring in a substantial amount of cash for themselves. There is a possibility that smaller cricket boards will have less control over the schedule, which will put them at a financial disadvantage.

Cricket in the Interest of Economic Growth

Cricket has the potential to be a driver of economic growth, particularly in countries that are still in the development stage. Several nations have utilized the sport as a tool to improve their infrastructure, provide new employment opportunities, and entice new investment.

Construction of the Stadium and Related Infrastructure:

Investing in the construction of cricket stadiums and associated infrastructure can result in the creation of employment opportunities and an increase in economic activity. These facilities can be put to a variety of uses, including hosting sporting events and entertainment performances as well as business gatherings.

The Promotion of Tourism:

A nation's profile on the international stage can be improved by hosting international cricket events, which in turn can increase the number of tourists that visit the area and strengthen the local tourism business. The marketing of tourism can result in increased economic activity as well as investment in other industries.

Programs for the Development of Young People:

Cricket training and development programs for young players can open doors to educational

and employment prospects. In addition to producing cricket players, they also create support workers and cricket administrators, both of which contribute to the environment of the sport.

Encouragement of the Use of Regional Brands:

The exposure of local brands and companies during cricket events can potentially contribute to increased recognition as well as increased revenue for those firms. This is beneficial to the local economy and assists in the growth of smaller businesses.

The economic relevance of cricket is a multidimensional and important component of the sport's overall significance. Ticket sales, sponsorship deals, merchandise opportunities, and TV rights are the primary revenue drivers for the sport. In addition to this, it fosters the growth of employment opportunities in a variety of industries, such as cricket, event management, the media, and retail. In addition, cricket stimulates economic activity related to tourism and hospitality, which is beneficial to the countries and towns that host cricket matches.

The economic success of cricket can be attributed in large part to the substantial role played by commercial activities. These include sponsorships, advertising, and leagues based on franchises.

However, there are significant economic inequalities present in the world of cricket, with more prosperous nations and boards of cricket enjoying a financial advantage over less influential boards. It is imperative that the economic potential of cricket be harnessed for the benefit of developing nations in order for these imbalances to be addressed and for economic growth to be promoted. Cricket has the potential to be a driving force for economic growth and progression. This may contribute to both the sport's worldwide appeal and the development of places that are in need of economic stimulation. This can be accomplished by constructing infrastructure, increasing tourism, and investing in youth development.

6.2 Development of infrastructure and facilities

The expansion of cricket's infrastructure and the number of available facilities is one of the most important factors in determining the future of the sport. The health of cricket's stadiums, training grounds, and other connected infrastructure is essential to the sport's continued popularity and financial viability. This essay of 1000 words dives into the relevance of infrastructure in cricket, including topics such as the construction of stadiums and training centers, as well as technological improvements and the role that hosting cricket events has in contributing to economic growth.

Before we begin:

It's not just about the players out on the field when it comes to cricket; the infrastructure and facilities that are there to back up the sport are just as important. The growth of cricket's infrastructure plays a critical part in determining the direction the sport will take in the years to come. This includes the construction of iconic stadiums that are used to host international matches as well as cutting-edge training facilities. This essay presents a comprehensive examination of the evolution of infrastructure and facilities in the sport of cricket. It emphasizes the value of well-maintained stadiums, the role of cutting-edge training centers, technological improvements, and the economic impact of hosting cricket events.

Construction and Reconstruction of the Stadium

The Most Important Part About Cricket:

The cricket stadium is the most important part of the game. These are the places that fans travel to in order to get a glimpse of their favored athletes and teams in action. The expansion of cricket's reach and appeal is dependent on the building of new stadiums and the refurbishment of existing ones.

Locations Across the Globe:

International cricket matches, such as Test matches, One Day Internationals (ODIs), and Twenty20 Internationals (T20Is), must take place in stadiums that are up to par with the requirements set forth by the international cricketing community. The development of these venues is essential to the upkeep of the sport's image because they stage matches that are seen by audiences from all over the world.

The Experience of the Fans and Their Capacity:

The experience that spectators have at stadiums needs to be improved. This encompasses things like the number of seats available, the level of comfort, the level of security, the viewing angles, and the availability of facilities like food and restrooms. The experience of being a spectator at a modern stadium is intentionally meant to be improved.

Implications for the Economy:

The building of new cricket stadiums or the refurbishment of existing ones has substantial repercussions for the local economy. These facilities frequently play host to domestic events, as well as franchise-based Twenty20 leagues and international matches. These events bring in spectators, sponsors, and broadcasters, which results in a significant increase in revenue.

Historically Significant and Iconic Reasons:

Cricket has a long and illustrious history, and some of the most famous stadiums in the sport are located all over the world, including Lord's in London, the Melbourne Cricket Ground (MCG) in Australia, and Eden Gardens in India. These arenas are a living memorial to the sport's illustrious history and continue to play host to important competitions.

Centers for Instruction That Are Completely Up to Date

The Development of Players:

In order to cultivate potential and make certain that players have access to the best resources with which to refine their abilities, the establishment of training centers of world-class caliber is essential. Cricket players can take advantage of the world-class instruction, facilities, and support staff that are offered at these centers.

Enhancement of Abilities:

Training facilities in modern sports are typically outfitted with cutting-edge technology to assist athletes in honing their talents. The majority of the time, these facilities consist of practice fields (both indoor and outdoor), gymnasiums, video analysis tools, and sports science labs.

Developing Young People:

Training centers are frequently the locations of programs for both grass-roots and youth development. These programs seek to discover and cultivate young talent by providing participants with the knowledge, experience, and chances they need to advance to higher levels of competition within their respective sports.

Rehabilitation of an Injury:

Injury recovery and player conditioning are two other areas that benefit from the presence of training centers. Physiotherapists and medical personnel who are trained professionals collaborate closely with athletes to ensure that the athletes are in the greatest possible physical condition.

Help with Schoolwork and Education in General:

Some training centers offer academic and educational support services, which can assist young cricket players in maintaining a healthy balance between their academic and athletic obligations. This ensures that gamers have a balanced and comprehensive growth experience.

Developments in the State of Technology

Technology Known as Hawk-Eye:

The use of the Hawk-Eye technology has become standard practice in the sport of cricket, particularly in the process of deciding Leg Before Wicket (LBW) appeals. This technology makes it easier for the umpires to make correct calls by following the path of the ball as it is tracked by more than one camera.

Stumps and Bails Illuminated by LEDs:

As part of an effort to improve the sight of dismissals, LED stumps and bails have been implemented. These advancements offer a distinct visual indicator when a wicket has been broken, which helps to reduce disagreements and debates.

Wearables and other methods of tracking players:

The player tracking system makes use of GPS and motion sensors to keep track of a player's whereabouts and performance while they are competing or participating in practice. The use of this data assists both the coaches and the athletes in honing their skills.

Tools for Analyzing the Pitch:

Tools for pitch analysis provide assistance to groundsmen in the process of preparing wickets that are even and consistent. The use of this technology guarantees that no one facet of the game will receive an advantage over another.

Analytics Performed in Real Time:

Viewers are provided with in-depth statistics and new perspectives on what's happening during broadcasts thanks to real-time data analytics. This makes for a more enjoyable viewing experience overall and provides a fresh option for fans to get involved.

The Potential Economic Effects of Hosting Cricket Matches

The Hospitality and Tourism Industry:

The staging of international cricket competitions, such as test series, one-day internationals, and Twenty20 internationals, brings in spectators and visitors. These tourists support the local tourism and hospitality businesses by staying in local hotels, eating at local restaurants, and taking part in other activities offered in the area.

Earnings from Customers:

Cricket boards and host towns should expect to see an increase in revenue as a result of hosting cricket events. The revenue generated from the sale of tickets, merchandising, and broadcasting rights, in addition to that generated from sponsorships and advertising, all contribute to the overall economic impact.

Possibilities for Employment:

Cricket tournaments offer employment opportunities in a variety of fields, such as event management, hospitality, transportation, and security, among others. Employment opportunities can also be generated through stadium maintenance, media coverage, and grounds management.

Encouragement of the Use of Regional Brands:

Cricket events promote local brands and enterprises, which in turn boosts the visibility of those entities and contributes to economic expansion. Not only cricket boards, but also local businesses, stand to benefit from this development.

The Development of Infrastructure:

The construction of cricket-related infrastructure may result from hosting cricket events. The

the general infrastructure of host cities can be improved by making improvements in areas such as transportation, lodging, and stadium facilities.

The expansion of cricket's infrastructure and the availability of facilities is essential to the sport's continued growth, popularity, and overall success. The development of cricket as a sport will be greatly influenced by factors such as new stadiums, training facilities, and technological advances. The development of players and the cultivation of talent is supported by stadiums that are kept in excellent condition and that have state-of-the-art training facilities. The level of precision and fairness of the game is increased by technological developments, which also engages fans in new ways.

In addition, hosting cricket competitions has a sizeable effect on the local economy, as it encourages tourism, results in the generation of income, results in the creation of job opportunities, helps promote local businesses, and leads to the construction of infrastructure. The economic repercussions of the game of cricket reach well beyond the boundary, showing the significant role that cricket plays in promoting economic growth and providing support for communities. The construction of infrastructure and facilities will continue to be vital for the future success of cricket and the sport's attractiveness on a worldwide scale as cricket continues its progression.

6.3 The role of cricket in education and youth development

Cricket, which is frequently seen as more than just a sport, plays a very important part in the education and growth of young people. Young people can benefit from the sport in a variety of ways, including the development of skills, the instillation of values, and the promotion of holistic growth. This essay of 1000 words examines the complex relationship between cricket, education, and the growth and development of young people. The author focuses on the positive effects of the sport on physical and mental growth, leadership and teamwork, academic advancement, and social integration.

Before we begin:

It has been known for a very long time that cricket is a sport that extends well beyond the confines of the pitch. It has the potential to enlighten, empower, and motivate today's young people. Cricket has a complex function in education and the development of young people, including but not limited to: intellectual and physical development; the cultivation of leadership and collaborative skills; the advancement of academic achievement; and the incorporation of young people into society. This article presents a comprehensive review of the impact that cricket has on education and youth development, with an emphasis on the positive influence that the sport has on young people.

The maturation of the body and the mind

Condition of the body:

Youth are more likely to be physically healthy if they play cricket. The sport needs quickness, strength, stamina, and coordination from its participants. Young people who play cricket on a regular basis are more likely to maintain a healthy and active lifestyle, which lowers their risk of obesity and other health problems associated with it.

Psychological fortitude:

The mental fortitude and focus required are put to the test by cricket. Mental toughness is improved by the requirement that players in the batting, bowling, and fielding positions maintain concentration when under duress. Young cricket players learn to handle tension, make snap judgments, and keep their cool in difficult situations.

Respect for Oneself and One's Work:

Cricket is a sport that requires a high level of discipline and a solid work ethic. Young athletes quickly understand the value of being on time, making a commitment, and making consistent effort. These principles apply not only to the game of cricket but also to other spheres of life, such as academics and personal relationships.

Respect for the Game and Sportsmanship:

The game of cricket encourages good sportsmanship and competitive fair play. The rules of the game place an emphasis on morality and candor. Cricket is a sport that teaches young players the importance of respecting their opponents, the umpires, and the overall spirit of the game.

Leadership and Collaboration in a Group

Competences in Leadership:

Young people have the opportunity to develop their leadership skills and take on roles such as team captain through the sport of cricket. As young leaders direct their teams, they develop a variety of leadership abilities, including the ability to make decisions, communicate effectively, and think strategically.

Collaboration and working well with others:

Cricket is a team sport, and being successful in the sport requires effective collaboration and teamwork from all players.

Young players develop the skills necessary to work together, communicate with one another, and provide support for one another, which fosters a sense of belonging and shared responsibility.

The Resolution of Conflict:

During games or practices, there is always the potential for arguments to break out. Young people who play cricket receive expertise in resolving disagreements, discovering solutions, and maintaining team cohesion, all of which are abilities that can be utilized in a variety of life scenarios.

Mentorship and Models to Look Up to:

Young cricketers frequently look up to more experienced players as examples of how to play the game. A significant contribution to the formation of young people's personalities is made by more experienced players' function as guides and mentors to younger players.

Progression in Education

Management of One's Time:

Managing your time well is essential if you want to play cricket and keep up with your studies. Young cricket players learn to balance their time between practicing, playing matches, and completing their schoolwork, which helps them build organizational skills that are beneficial to their academic careers.

Respect for Authority and Personal Accountability:

The level of self-control that is developed through regular practice of cricket is transferable to one's academic duties. Young people are aware of the significance of meeting their academic commitments, including finishing their assignments, going to their classes, and so on.

Programs to Assist with Academics

Young cricket players are supported academically by a number of organizations and clubs dedicated to the sport of cricket. These programs provide adolescents with tutoring, study materials, and other services to assist them in excelling in their academic pursuits.

Opportunities for Scholarships and Furthering Education:

Young cricketers who demonstrate exceptional talent and potential have the possibility to receive financial aid and scholarships from cricket governing bodies, clubs, and institutions.

The financial burden of obtaining a higher education may be reduced as a result of these alternatives.

Integration into society

The importance of diversity and inclusion:

The sport of cricket brings together people from a wide range of backgrounds, which helps to promote a spirit of acceptance and inclusion. Because of the sport's widespread popularity, young players are able to communicate with competitors of other cultures, which encourages variety and tolerance.

Participation in the Community:

Local communities are frequently involved in cricket competitions, regardless of whether the tournament is on a local or international level. These encounters help young people develop a sense of community and belonging to a group to which they belong.

Programs for the Development of Young People:

There are several cricket boards and organizations that operate youth development programs that give participants the opportunity to grow as individuals, become leaders, and serve their communities. These programs allow young cricketers the opportunity to give back to their communities.

Motivating Factors: Inspiration and Aspiration

Cricketers who achieve success in their careers frequently serve as role models for younger generations. Their successes encourage younger generations to go for their goals, set their sights high, and put in a lot of effort to attain them, not only in athletics but also in life.

Cricket has a diverse function in education and the development of young people, including but not limited to the following: mental and physical development, leadership and teamwork, academic advancement, and social integration. Young people who participate in sports are given the opportunity to develop important life skills such as self-discipline, teamwork, mental toughness, and the ability to resolve conflicts. In addition to this, it motivates students to make academic progress and provides exceptional talent with scholarships and other educational opportunities.

In addition, the sport of cricket encourages diversity, inclusivity, and community engagement. This helps young people feel like they belong and are accepted by their peers.

The sport motivates young people to have lofty goals and offers them with role models who are examples of how to achieve those goals via hard effort, dedication, and perseverance.

The sport of cricket has an everlasting relevance in terms of molding the lives and futures of young people all over the world, and the sport's impact on education and youth development is a witness to the sport's ongoing growth and evolution.

Chapter 7

The Modern Era

The "Modern Era" is a time period in history that is defined by substantial econom-ical, technological, and cultural transformations that have created the contemporary world. These transformations have been referred to as "modernization." The Modern Era is investigated in depth throughout this three thousand word essay, which dives into its beginnings, significant milestones, and the manner in which it has transformed human society, politics, the economy, and culture. In addition to this, we will talk about the opportunities and difficulties that were brought about by this age, as well as the impacts that are still having an effect on our world now.

Before we begin:

The modern era, often known as modernity, was a time of dramatic upheaval and development

that had a significant impact on human society, politics, the economy, and culture in ways that can be felt even today. This time period marks a considerable break from more conventional ways of living and thinking. It is denoted by a number of notable milestones and developments that have had far-reaching effects on society as a whole. In this essay of 3,000 words, we will investigate the Modern Era, discussing its beginnings, defining characteristics, and the impact it has had on the world as we know it today.

The Beginnings of the Contemporary Era

The 14th through the 17th centuries are known as the Renaissance:

The cultural movement known as the Renaissance had its origins in Italy but quickly expanded throughout the rest of Europe. The renaissance was characterized by a renewed interest in the arts, sciences, and humanism. It placed an emphasis on individualism, rationalism, and the rediscovering of classical knowledge. This cultural revolution was crucial in laying the groundwork for contemporary thought intellectually.

The 15th to the 17th century are known as the Age of Exploration:

During the Age of Exploration, numerous European nations set sail on maritime missions with the goals of discovering, colonizing, and establishing commercial relationships with lands located outside Europe. The discovery of the New World and new trade routes that resulted from this era made it easier for people all over the world to trade commodities and ideas with one another.

From the 16th to the 18th centuries, the Scientific Revolution:

The work of scientists like Galileo Galilei, Isaac Newton, and Johannes Kepler helped usher in a new era of understanding of the natural world, which is known as the Scientific Revolution. The application of knowledge was revolutionized by the Scientific Method, which consists of empirical observation and experimental investigation.

The Enlightenment occurred during the 17th and 18th centuries:

The Enlightenment was a philosophical and intellectual movement that placed an emphasis on reason, the rights of the individual, and the quest of knowledge. Concepts such as democracy, freedom of opinion, and separation of powers were championed by thinkers such as John Locke, Voltaire, and Jean-Jacques Rousseau, who were instrumental in building the framework for contemporary political and social ideas.

These events laid the groundwork for the fundamental shifts that would come to define the Modern Era as we know it. In the following parts, we will discuss the significant landmarks that have occurred throughout history as well as the impact that modernity has had on numerous elements of human life.

Transformations in Society and the Economy

The Industrial Revolution, which occurred between the 18th and 19th centuries:

The mechanization of many industries, the proliferation of factories, and the spread of urbanization were all hallmarks of the Industrial Revolution, which was a defining point in the Modern Era. This transition had a significant effect on work, production, and living conditions, and it was ultimately responsible for the development of the modern labor force and the ascendance of capitalism as the preeminent form of economic organization.

Population Movement and Urbanization:

People moved from rural areas to urban areas in pursuit of jobs as a direct result of the fast urbanization and industrialization that occurred throughout the Modern Era. This resulted in huge population migrations. This tendency continues to have an influence on contemporary demographics as well as living habits.

Colonialism and imperialism: both were evil:

The modern era was the pinnacle of colonial expansion and imperialism on the part of European nations. These activities had far-reaching effects on the social, political, and economic systems of the territories that were colonized, and the legacy they left behind continues to shape geopolitics and socioeconomic inequities on a worldwide scale.

Developments in the State of Technology

The Development of New Technologies:

The Modern Era was marked by tremendous technological developments that radically altered the ways in which manufacturing, transportation, and communication were conducted. People's ways of living and working were fundamentally altered as a result of the invention of the telegraph, the steam engine, electricity, and the internal combustion engine.

Revolution in Information Technology:

The development of the printing press by Johannes Gutenberg in the 15th century was a game-changer for the dissemination of information and knowledge since it made it easier for people to get their hands on it. The advent of the internet, computers, and mobile technologies in the contemporary age significantly increased the dissemination of knowledge. This was made possible by the digital revolution.

Recent Developments in Medicine:

The development of modern medicine, including antibiotics, vaccinations, and techniques for surgical procedures, has significantly increased the average human life expectancy and significantly decreased mortality rates caused by infectious diseases. The procedures and results of modern healthcare are still being influenced by these developments.

The Exploration of Space:

The Modern Era was characterized by humankind's expansion beyond Earth's surface, with the space race in the middle of the 20th century culminating with the Apollo 11 landing on the moon in 1969. The exploration of space continues to be a demonstration of the technological might and insatiable curiosity of humans.

Transformations on Both the Political and Social Fronts

Movements for Democratic Societies:

During the Modern Era, democratic institutions and ideas began to expand throughout the world. Both the American Revolution (1775-1783) and the French Revolution (1789-1799) served as catalysts for the development of democratic institutions, with the ideas of liberty, equality, and fraternity coming to the forefront of society as a result.

Movements Concerning Civil Rights:

The fight for civil rights, equality, and social justice was one of the most significant motifs that emerged throughout the course of the Modern Era. Movements such as the American Civil Rights Movement, the Indian Independence Movement led by Mahatma Gandhi, and the anti-apartheid movement in South Africa all aimed to overcome the structural prejudice and inequality that existed in their respective countries.

The Rise of Nationalism and the Decolonization Process:

The emergence of nationalism and the subsequent decolonization of a large number of countries in Asia, Africa, and the Middle East are two of the defining characteristics of the Modern Era. The clamor for self-determination and independence was a significant factor in the transformation of the political landscape and the development of international relations.

The era of globalization:

The modern period has witnessed a level of globalization that has never been seen before, with increasing interconnection, higher trade, and increased cultural exchange between nations. Integration of economies, communication networks, and transportation systems has resulted in far-reaching ramifications for politics, culture, and economics.

Changes in Culture as well as the Intellectual Landscape

Culture and the Arts:

Art and culture underwent profound shifts during the Modern Era, as a result of the rise of artistic movements such as Romanticism, Realism, Impressionism, and Modernism, which rethought the meaning of artistic expression. The alterations in creative expression that have taken place over the years continue to have an impact on modern art and culture.

Movements in Literature:

Literary groups such as Romanticism and the Beat Generation were responsible for redefining literature by questioning established canons and investigating alternative modes of expression. The literary world and the human experience were profoundly influenced as a result of these revolutions.

The Press and Other Forms of Communication:

The modern era was marked by the introduction of numerous innovations in communication and media. The proliferation of mass media such as radio, television, and the internet ushered in a new era in the dissemination of information and the consumption of forms of entertainment.

The Opportunities and Obstacles Facing Us in the Modern Era

Concerns Regarding the Environment:

Pollution, deforestation, and climate change are just a few of the environmental problems that have been exacerbated by the rapid pace of industrialization and technological growth. In this day and age, finding solutions to these problems is an extremely pressing subject.

Inequalities on a Global Scale:

Although the modern period has brought about tremendous improvements, it has also increased global inequities. Disparities in wealth, access to resources, and opportunities continue to be an issue despite the fact that the modern era has brought about significant achievements.

The Disruption Caused by Technology

The rapid pace of technological progress in the modern era has caused disruptions in a variety of different businesses, ranging from retail to manufacturing. The problem lies in adjusting to these shifts in the labor market while simultaneously guaranteeing a fair transition for employees.

Problems of Integrity and Conscience:

The advent of modernity has given rise to a number of moral and ethical conundrums that are associated with the growth of science, the protection of personal privacy, and the appropriate application of technology. Finding a happy medium between technological advancement and moral principles is a constant struggle.

Effects that the Contemporary Era Continues to Have

The Modern Era has left an indelible impression on the modern world, with many of its consequences continuing to have an impact in the present day and age.

Systems of the Economy:

The dominance of capitalism and market-oriented economies that came about as a result of the industrial revolution continues to shape economic systems all over the world.

Political Methodologies:

The ideas of democracy, human rights, and self-determination, which came to the forefront throughout the Modern Era, continue to have an impact on both the political systems that exist and the relationships that exist between nations.

The era of globalization:

The interconnectedness and interdependence of nations that are characteristics of globalization continue to be a defining aspect of the modern world, having an impact on commerce, culture, and politics.

The Advancement of Technology:

The continuous speed of technological improvement in the Modern Era continues to drive innovation and influence the way in which we live, work, and connect with one another.

The current era, known as the Modern Era, is characterized by a period of tremendous change and transformation, which is distinguished by important advancements in a variety of facets of human life. The Modern Era has left an indelible mark on the world we live in today, leaving its mark on everything from the Renaissance to the Industrial Revolution, from democratic movements to globalization. It has opened doors as well as closed them, and its repercussions continue to mold the modern world in ways that are intricate, diverse, and far-reaching. It is vital to have a solid understanding of the Modern Era in order to know the roots of our contemporary society as well as the issues we confront in the 21st century.

7.1 The impact of technology on the game

Cricket, which was originally a relaxing game enjoyed in the picturesque English countryside, has grown into a high-tech extravaganza as a result of a variety of technical developments that have completely revolutionized the sport. This article of 1000 words investigates the tremendous impact that technology has had on cricket. Topics discussed include the Decision Review System (DRS), Hawk-Eye, Snickometer, LED stumps and bails, wearables, and the role that data analytics play. The game has been completely transformed as a result of these advances, which have resulted in increased precision, additional tools for analysis, and an overall enhancement of the experience for both players and viewers.

Before we begin:

Cricket is a sport that has always placed a significant emphasis on history and tradition. Nevertheless, in the previous decades, technology has brought about significant changes in the way the game is played, officiated, and enjoyed by fans. These changes have been brought about by technological advancements. It is impossible to emphasize how much of an impact technology has had on cricket, since advancements in the field have helped to make the game more balanced, analytical, and entertaining. This essay digs into the game-changing technology that have altered cricket, highlighting the roles that the Decision Review System (DRS), Hawk-Eye, Snickometer, LED stumps and bails, wearables, and data analytics have played in the evolution of the sport.

The Decision Review System, sometimes known as the DRS

Tracking the Ball using Hawk-Eye:

The Hawk-Eye technology is an essential component of the Defense Radar System (DRS). Hawk-Eye is able to make accurate projections of where the ball would have gone if it hadn't hit the batsman or the defender because it employs a system of numerous cameras to trace the course of the ball. The decisions that are made about LBW (leg before wicket) and caught-behind dismissals have been altered as a result of this technology.

In this edition of Ultra Edge and Snickometer:

The technology known as Ultra Edge and Snickometer are utilized to determine whether or not the ball has made contact with the bat or pad, respectively. These advancements allow for a more precise portrayal of whether or not a batsman has been dismissed, particularly in the case of caught-behind dismissals.

The Hotspot:

Hot Spot is able to detect the heat generated by the impact of a ball hitting a bat or pad by using thermal imaging technology. This assists in evaluating the presence of minuscule touches that might not be visible to the human eye.

The DRS gives players the ability to question the choices made by the umpires, which leads to a higher level of accuracy and fairness in the game. It has resulted in fewer contentious situations and increased the quality of decisions made by the umpires generally.

The Hawk's Eye

LBW Determinations:

By providing a visual picture of the ball's trajectory, Hawk-Eye has substantially enhanced the accuracy of leg before wicket judgments. It has helped to make leg before wicket rulings that are more fair by reducing the number of errors that occur while determining whether or not the ball would have hit the stumps.

Challenges from DRS:

The ball-tracking technology developed by Hawk-Eye lies at the heart of DRS's issues. It is used by the players and teams to review the judgments made by the umpires, which adds a strategic and dramatic element to the game.

Both Amusement and Interpretation:

The graphical depictions of the ball's path that are provided by Hawk-Eye have become a staple part of broadcasts of cricket matches. The predicted course and the analysis of the trajectory of deliveries are both entertaining for fans to see.

The Snickometer:

Another piece of technology that has helped enhance decision-making in the sport of cricket is called a snickometer. This instrument can determine whether the ball has touched the bat or the pad. It does this by analyzing the sound captured by the microphone attached to the stump, listening for the sound made when the ball brushes up against the bat. The Snickometer has developed into a vital piece of equipment for both cricket umpires and broadcasters as a result of its exceptional utility in verifying caught-behind dismissals.

Stumps and Bails Lit Up by LEDs

The game of cricket now features more visually arresting elements thanks to the implementation of LED stumps and bails. Because of these advancements, it is now simpler for umpires to assess whether a player was dismissed by run-out or stumping. When the bails are removed, a clear indicator that a wicket has been shattered is provided by the light that shines from within them. This method guarantees that choices on close run-outs are made with precision, hence removing ambiguity and improving the accuracy of run-out decisions.

Things to wear

Wearable technology, such as fitness trackers and smartwatches, are frequently utilized by modern cricket players as a means of monitoring their physical performance. The information gleaned from these gadgets, which track variables such as a user's heart rate, distance traveled, and amount of energy expended, is extremely beneficial to both players and coaches. Wearable technology assists athletes in more successfully managing their fitness and training routines, which ultimately improves their performance on the field.

The Analyses of Data

In the sport of cricket, data analytics has emerged as a game-changing innovation that offers players, teams, and spectators invaluable insights. Collecting and analyzing a variety of statistics and performance measures for the purpose of enhancing decision-making is entailed in this process. The following are some of the most important components of data analytics in cricket:

Analysis of the Player's Performance:

Data analytics are used by teams to evaluate player performance and to pinpoint players' areas of strength and weakness. This information is utilized in the process of making tactical decisions regarding the make-up of the team, the batting order, and the fielding positions.

Analysis of the Competitor:

Data analytics is utilized to research the strategies and vulnerabilities of one's opponents. Teams make use of this information to design strategies and tactics for the game that take advantage of the weaknesses of their opponents.

Management of the Workload Carried by Players:

The use of data analytics allows for better monitoring of player weariness and workload. It provides insights on when players need to rest and when they may push harder in training and matches, hence lowering the chance of injuries that could occur.

Participation from Fans:

The experience of the fans has also been improved thanks to data analytics. It gives viewers with in-depth information and insights while they are watching the broadcast, which enables fans to participate with the game on a deeper level.

Disputes and Obstacles to Overcome

The Call of the Umpire:

The idea of "Umpire's Call" in leg before wicket rulings, in which the on-field decision stands even if the ball-tracking technology reveals that the ball would have clipped the stumps, has been the subject of much debate and controversy.

The Dependability of Technology:

There have been instances in which the accuracy and dependability of technology, notably in the areas of DRS and ball-tracking, have been called into question. Continued difficulties include calibration and maintaining consistency.

Influence on the Traditional Methods of Umpiring:

There are others who believe that traditional umpires and their judgment have become less important in games as a result of the greater use of technology in the decision-making process.

Technology has undeniably had a significant and positive impact on cricket, which has improved accuracy, provided new tools for analysis, and improved the whole experience for both players and fans. The game has been changed via the introduction of new technologies such as the Decision Review System (DRS), Hawk-Eye, Snickometer, LED stumps and bails, wearables, and data analytics. These advancements have made the game more balanced, interactive, and data-driven.

Despite the fact that there are still issues to be resolved and debates to be had, the influence of technology on cricket has been overwhelmingly good. Cricket is likely to witness even more developments as technology continues to advance, all of which will serve to further enhance the sport and attract fans all around the world. The introduction of new technologies has resulted in an overall improvement to the cricketing experience as well as a sustained increase in the popularity of the sport.

7.2 Evolution of formats: Test, One Day, and T20

The format of cricket, a sport that has a long and illustrious history, has been subject to tremendous change during the course of its existence. This essay of 1000 words examines the history, characteristics, and impact of each cricket format, ranging from the more traditional Test cricket to the limited-overs versions of One Day Internationals (ODIs) and Twenty20 (T20) cricket. The traditional format of cricket is the Test match. We are going to delve into the ways in which various formats have molded the sport, created unique viewing opportunities, and broadened cricket's popularity on a worldwide scale.

Before we begin:

Cricket is a sport that is well-known for its extensive history, long-standing customs, and many playing formats. Cricket has developed throughout the years to accommodate a variety of preferences and audiences, which has led to the creation of three basic formats: test cricket, one-day internationals (also known as ODIs), and twenty-over cricket (often known as T20 cricket). In this essay, we will investigate the development of various formats, focusing on their individual characteristics as well as the historical relevance and influence they have had on the sport of cricket.

Cricket with a Test

The First Men and Their Significance in History:

Test cricket is the version of the game that has been played for the longest time and adheres to the most rules.

It was first played in the 19th century, and it gained its name from the fact that "Test matches" were thought to be the pinnacle of a cricket player's ability to demonstrate both talent and endurance. At the Melbourne Cricket Ground in the year 1877, England and Australia competed in the very first Test match that had ever been played.

Principal Attributes:

Prolonged Timeframe:

The duration of a test match is limited to a maximum of five days, and during that time, each team bats twice. Players are put to the test of their endurance as well as their talent and mental fortitude with this format.

Ball in Red:

The red cricket ball used in test cricket is thought to provide bowlers with extra movement, particularly when the circumstances are favorable.

Traditional white wines include:

In test matches, it is customary for players to wear white uniforms, which contributes to the classic and enduring allure of the competition.

Strategic Shades of Grey:

The format of a test match in cricket allows for intricate tactical clashes, with each team adopting a diverse array of tactics in an effort to win or draw.

The Influence and Significance of:

Test cricket continues to be the most competitive form of the game, with numerous records, long-standing customs, and important moments permanently inscribed into its legacy. It has given the world players of legend and matches of iconic status. In spite of the popularity of limited-overs cricket, "Test" matches will always have a unique place in cricket purists' affections, and they will continue to occupy a pivotal position in the sport's annual schedule.

One-Day Internationals are abbreviated as "ODIs"

The First Men and Their Significance in History:

In the 1960s, in response to the demand for shorter and more spectator-friendly contests, the idea of playing cricket with a fixed number of overs was developed.

In 1971, England and Australia competed against one another in the inaugural official One Day International match. One-day internationals are intended to be a more streamlined and approachable form of cricket that can appeal to a wider audience.

Principal Attributes:

Only a Few Spots Left:

Due to the fact that one-day internationals have a maximum limit of 50 overs each side, matches frequently last for close to eight hours. This time duration makes one-day internationals more approachable for players as well as spectators.

Ball of White:

White cricket balls are used in one-day internationals because they are easier to see under floodlights. This allows for day-night matches to be played.

Clothing in Various Colors:

Players in one-day internationals wear colored apparel, which boosts the game's visual appeal and makes it more suitable for broadcast on television.

Restrictions on the Playing Field:

ODIs contain fielding limits, notably the powerplay overs, which limit the number of fielders allowed outside the 30-yard circle. These restrictions are designed to encourage more aggressive play on the field.

The Influence and Significance of:

One-day internationals have been a significant contributor to the spread of cricket around the world. The limited-overs style offers a version of the game that is both fun and condensed, making it more accessible to a wider audience. One of the athletic events that attracts the most viewers around the world is the 50-over World Cup, which takes place once every four years. The One-Day International (ODI) format has been responsible for producing classic moments, renowned players, and memorable matchups, all of which have captivated cricket fans all over the world.

Cricket's Twenty20 (T20) format

The First Men and Their Significance in History:

The Twenty20 format is the newest of the three basic formats, and it was developed as a solution to meet the demand for cricket matches that are both shorter and more exciting. In 2005, New Zealand and Australia competed against each other in the first international Twenty20 match. The Twenty20 style of cricket was developed to be the most enjoyable for spectators as well as the most profitable on a business level.

Principal Attributes:

Each side gets twenty overs:

T20 matches are very condensed and action-packed due to the fact that each team only gets 20 overs to bat.

Garments with Vivid Colors:

Players don garb that is brightly colored and often individualized, embracing a look that is more contemporary and aesthetically pleasing.

Floodlit Matches and Day-Night Matches:

The majority of Twenty20 matches are played under lights, which creates an exciting environment, particularly for games played in the evening or at night.

Powerplay Opportunities and Fielding Restrictions:

Powerplays are available for both the batting team and the fielding team in Twenty20 cricket, which encourages aggressive and imaginative strategies.

The Influence and Significance of:

The introduction of Twenty20 cricket was a significant step forward for the sport. It has expanded the reach of cricket to new audiences, particularly in countries that do not traditionally play the game. The emphasis placed on entertainment and excitement has led to a transformation in the way cricket is played as a result of the format. Cricket has become a year-round spectacle thanks to the proliferation of Twenty20 leagues like the Indian Premier League (IPL) and the Big Bash League, both of which have seen significant commercial success. The Twenty20 World Cup has contributed to the format's continued rise in popularity, helping players and teams achieve the status of celebrities.

The Evolving Pathway of Formats: A Revolutionary Experience

The progression of cricket formats from Test cricket to One-Day Internationals and Twenty20 has been a transformative journey that has shaped the appeal and reach of the game. T20 cricket is the most recent format to have emerged. The following is an explanation of how this change has affected the world of cricket:

Multiple Types of Readers:

Different types of audiences are catered to by the various presentation forms. Test cricket is popular among cricket purists and those who are more knowledgeable about the sport. Those in search of amusement that can be completed in a single day frequent ODIs. The Twenty20 format of cricket is incredibly popular, particularly among those in their twenties and thirties.

The era of globalization:

T20 cricket in particular has been a major contributor to the sport's expansion into new markets throughout the world. Cricket has seen an increase in popularity as a result of the efforts of several leagues, such as the Indian Premier League (IPL), which have helped to make the sport more widely available.

Prosperity in Financial Aspects:

The popularity of limited-overs cricket, in particular T20 leagues, has resulted in significant increases in revenue. These leagues have also attracted investments, sponsorships, and media attention, which has benefited players, boards, and the whole infrastructure of the sport.

Recent Developments in Technology:

As a result of the game being played in shorter formats, technological advancements have been made in areas such as enhanced cricket equipment, improved ground facilities, and cutting-edge broadcasting. This has further contributed to an improved experience for cricket fans.

Adaptability of the Player:

Because players have been required to adjust to various formats of the game, a new breed of adaptable cricketers who are able to excel in all variations of the sport has emerged. Because of this adaptability, the level of international cricket has significantly improved.

Value in terms of Entertainment:

Cricket's entertainment value has increased thanks to the development of new forms, which has resulted in an increase in the number of viewers as well as a more active fan base.

The flexibility of cricket to adapt to changing times and preferences is shown in the game's progression through its various formats, which range from the time-honored and lasting game of Test cricket to the fast-paced and commercially viable game of Twenty20 cricket. Each cricket format has its own set of distinguishing traits, as well as its own historical relevance and influence on the sport as a whole. Together, they add to the all-encompassing and multidimensional appeal of cricket, which is one of the main reasons why it is one of the most popular and revered games in the world. Cricket continues to develop, continue to capture fans on a global scale, and bring people together no matter where they are located in the world. This is true whether fans are taking in the ageless elegance of a Test match, the high stakes drama of an ODI, or the explosive excitement of a Twenty20 competition.

7.3 The rise of franchise leagues and their influence

The rise of franchise leagues as a dominant factor in the landscape of modern sports is unmistakable. The landscape of sports has been drastically transformed as a result of the proliferation of leagues that feature privately owned clubs that compete to represent particular cities or regions. This study examines the development of franchise leagues, as well as its historical beginnings, important characteristics, and significant influence on contemporary sports, including their impact on player careers, fan engagement, and the economics of the sports industry. Specifically, this investigation focuses on how franchise leagues have affected player careers, fan engagement, and the economics of the sports industry.

Defining Franchise Leagues and Organizations

Private Property Rights:

The teams in franchise leagues are privately owned, and individuals or corporate entities can purchase the rights to run a franchise in a certain territory by paying a franchise fee. Franchise leagues are often seen in sports. In contrast to this, the conventional club-based model, in which teams are frequently owned or administered by national associations or member-based organizations, continues to be prevalent today.

Team Ownership and Independent Decision-Making:

The franchise owners enjoy a great degree of autonomy, which includes control over the general operations of the team as well as influence over the recruitment of players and coaching staff. They have the capacity to develop a distinctive identity and brand for the squad, which can be honed to optimize its marketability and attractiveness to businesses.

Representation of Geographic Areas:

Most of the time, the teams that compete in franchise leagues represent particular cities or areas. Fans develop strong local attachments and a sense of regional pride as a result of this geographical representation, which in turn helps to establish a sense of community and identity.

The process of commercialization, as well as branding:

In franchise leagues, branding and commercialization are given top priority. Teams frequently have unique names, logos, and color schemes, all of which contribute to the marketability of the teams and the level of fan involvement they receive. The league's general appeal and economic value are both increased as a result of this branding strategy.

Mobility of the Player:

Franchise leagues encourage player mobility by holding drafts, transfers, and auctions. This makes it possible for sportsmen to move more freely between different teams. This mobility ensures that the player landscape will be dynamic and constantly growing.

The Beginnings and Rapid Development of Franchise Leagues

Leagues in the Americas:

The National Basketball Association (NBA) is the most well-known example of the franchise league model that is prevalent in the United States. The National Basketball Association (NBA) was established in 1946, and since then it has been essential in increasing the influence and reach of the franchise model throughout the sporting world.

Spread Around the World:

There have been franchise leagues established in countries other than the United States. Other countries have followed suit by establishing leagues for a number of sports that are centered on the concept of franchises. This model has gained hold in a variety of sports all over the world, including cricket with the Indian Premier League (IPL), soccer with the Major League Soccer (MLS), and other sports.

Influence on the Economy:

The commercial success of franchise leagues has had a considerable impact on the economy, as seen by the fact that it has attracted investments, sponsorships, and attention from the media. Because of this, the general infrastructure of these leagues, as well as that of the entire sports sector, has been strengthened as a result.

Impact on the Professional Careers of Players

Exposure to the World:

Players have access to a global platform thanks to the proliferation of franchise leagues, particularly in the sports of cricket and basketball, which has increased their reach and visibility beyond the borders of their home nations. Players from other countries have risen to the status of sports icons on a global scale, garnering huge support from fans all around the world.

Rewards in terms of Money:

The players in franchise leagues typically receive huge financial advantages, including increased pay as well as significant chances for endorsement deals. For instance, the Indian Premier League is well-known for the rich player contracts that it offers.

Mobility of the Player:

By holding drafts, auctions, and trades, franchise leagues make it easier for players to move across the league. Because of the constant mobility of athletes, players are exposed to a variety of places, cultures, and coaching philosophies, which eventually helps them improve their skills and their capacity to adapt.

Management of Longevity Risks and Injuries:

Due to the highly competitive and rigorous nature of franchise leagues, there has been a shift toward placing a higher emphasis on the health and longevity of players. The careers of athletes can be lengthened thanks to the investment that clubs make in player conditioning, rehabilitation programs, and injury management.

Participation from Fans and Ownership of Media

Loyalty to One's Own Region:

Regional allegiances are given a higher priority in franchise leagues, which feature clubs that represent particular cities or areas. Fans have a strong feeling of local identification and regional pride as a result of the geographic representation of their favorite teams.

Experiences for Fans:

Franchise leagues make investments to improve the fan experience by providing engaging activities, themed matchdays, and promotions. The goal is to make attending or viewing games an experience that is both memorable and captivating on a deeper level.

Broadcasting and the Rights of the Media:

The media rights and broadcasting partnerships that franchise leagues demand are considerable, allowing them to reach audiences all over the world through television and digital channels. Because of the proliferation of streaming platforms and digital collaborations, the influence on the field of sports broadcasting has been nothing short of revolutionary.

Engaging with Social Media and Digital Technologies:
The use of social media, digital platforms, and interactive material are some of the ways that franchise leagues actively communicate with their fans. They provide access to behind-the-scenes action, unique content, and interactive elements, all of which contribute to an improved experience for the fan base as a whole.

The Business Side of Sports

The process of commercialization
The commercialization of franchise leagues is a top priority, and they capitalize on the money

earned from TV partnerships, sponsorships, item sales, and franchise fees. These monetary resources help to the leagues' ability to continue growing in a sustainable manner.

Opportunities for Business Expansion:
Franchise leagues are responsible for the creation of prospects for expansion. As a result, new franchises are frequently launched, and considerable profits are made from the sale of franchise rights. The overall financial well-being of the leagues receives a boost as a result of this expansion.

Advantages to the Local Economy for Host Cities:
Cities that host franchise-based leagues see an increase in economic benefits, including as increased tourism and spending in the local community, as well as earnings tied to stadiums. These leagues provide a contribution to the economic growth of the cities and regions in which they are hosted.

Creating New Jobs:
Franchise leagues generate employment opportunities not only for athletes but also for support staff, such as coaches, physiotherapists, marketing teams, and stadium personnel. Franchise leagues also provide opportunities for spectators. The creation of new jobs has a beneficial effect on the economies of both the community and the area.

Disputes and Obstacles to Overcome
Although franchise leagues have many benefits to offer, they are also plagued by difficulties and issues that need to be taken into mind.

Differences in Financial Status:
Some franchise leagues have been called out for the financial inequalities that exist between their clubs, which can have an effect on the competitive balance as well as the integrity of the competition as a whole.

A Case of Player Fatigue:
It is possible for players to become burned out due to the rigorous schedules of franchise leagues, which then limits their participation in international or other domestic events. The management of the workloads of the players becomes an important matter.

Player Auctions and the Dynamics of the Market:

The player auction system, which is common in franchise leagues, has come under attention for the impact it has on player values, market-driven dynamics, and the possibility that players would be exploited.

The battle between commercialization and tradition:

The franchise leagues' strong emphasis on commercialization and branding has sparked disputes concerning the perceived overemphasis on profit, as well as the erosion of traditional athletic ideals. These debates have been sparked by the fact that these leagues place a great emphasis on commercialization and branding.

The sports industry has been completely transformed by the introduction of franchise leagues, which have made new opportunities, experiences, and challenges available. They have changed the trajectory of player careers, increased fan involvement, and revolutionized the economics of the sports industry. The significance of franchise leagues extends beyond the boundaries of individual leagues; they establish new benchmarks for the industry of sports business and act as a template for other sports organizations to emulate. As these leagues continue to develop and expand, they will have an impact on the future of sports in ways that have not yet been fully revealed. As a result, the world of athletics will continue to be exciting, dynamic, and innovative.

Chapter 8

Global Tensions and Diplomacy through Cricket

Cricket, sometimes known as the "gentleman's game," is a sport that is played across national boundaries and cultural boundaries, and it has captured the hearts of millions of people all over the world. Cricket, which on the surface may appear to be nothing more than a game, has repeatedly been used as a platform for diplomacy and the resolution of conflicts, particularly in countries where emotions run particularly high. In this essay of 3,000 words, we will investigate the historical and contemporary instances of how cricket has played a role in alleviating global tensions, developing diplomacy, and bringing nations together. In particular, we will focus on the role that cricket has played in bringing India and Pakistan together. We will investigate the role that this sport has had as a conduit for diplomatic communication, whether it be in the context of relations between India and Pakistan, apartheid-era South Africa, or other geopolitical crises.

The Power of Cricket to Bring People Together

Because of cricket's distinct status as a global sport with a long and illustrious history and a devoted fanbase, it has been able to traverse both political and cultural divides. Cricket, in contrast to many other sports, can lay claim to fans on every continent, making it a worldwide phenomenon that carries enormous cultural weight. Because of its vast appeal and the widespread love that people feel for playing the game, it has become a great unifying factor.

Cricket has frequently been a cause for nations to feel a sense of pride, acting as a representation of their national identity and bringing them moments of joy and celebration. It bridges the gaps that may occur between people as a result of other parts of life and brings them together. Cricket matches, regardless of whether they are played on an international, national, or even a local scale, have the potential to bring communities and nations closer together by developing a sense of belonging and a common purpose.

Contextualization of the Past

The early days of cricket can be seen as the beginning of the sport's historical significance as a medium for diplomacy and the resolution of conflicts. As a result of the growth and influence of the British Empire in the 19th century, the sport of cricket was introduced to many different parts of the world, turning it into an instrument of colonialism.

Cricket, on the other hand, became a method by which nations could demonstrate their national identities and express their political objectives as they earned their independence.

When Australia and England competed against one another in the "Bodyline" series at the beginning of the 20th century, it was one of the earliest examples of how cricket might be used for diplomatic purposes. The strategies that England employed led to diplomatic difficulties between the two countries, with the Australian government voicing its concerns about the situation as a result of England's actions. This occurrence brought to light the potential for a cricket series to have diplomatic repercussions and generated discussions over good sportsmanship and ethical conduct within the sport.

India and Pakistan Engaged in Some Diplomatic Cricket Action

The cricket rivalry between India and Pakistan is one of the few examples of cricket's diplomatic power that is as profound and as generally known as it is. Cricket has been utilized as a method of interaction and discussion between these two adjacent nations for decades. These nations have a history of political clashes and tensions, but cricket has been used as a way to bring them together.

The Game of Cricket During Times of War:

Even during periods of heightened political tension, India and Pakistan have frequently continued to engage in cricketing interactions with one another. Both countries are able to compete and interact with one another in a more cordial manner because to the neutral ground provided by the cricket field, which reveals a more positive aspect of their relationship.

Cricket Matches as Opportunities for Bilateral Cooperation:

Cricket matches between India and Pakistan have, on occasion, served as a platform for bilateral endeavors to enhance the two countries' diplomatic ties. The top officials from both nations have met in a less formal setting during sporting events, which they have attended.

Diplomacy with the Public:

The cricket competition between India and Pakistan has also acted as a sort of public diplomacy, making it possible for the people of both countries to communicate with one another and bond over a common interest. The other side is given a face and connections between individuals are fostered as a result.

Cricket as a Force for Harmony:

Tournaments called "Cricket for Peace" are one of the many activities that have been planned as part of a larger effort to foster coexistence and communication between the two countries. Cricket serves as the vehicle through which these activities bring people together and highlight the similarities that exist between the various cultures.

The Apartheid System and the Isolation of South Africa

Cricket was an important part of the resistance movement in South Africa during the time of apartheid. During the time of apartheid, South Africa was socially and politically isolated on a global scale. One of the primary methods of protest against the discriminatory practices of the country was to boycott its athletic events.

The Boycott of Cricket:

Because to the worldwide boycott, South Africa's national and international cricket teams were effectively barred from participating in international play. This boycott was one facet of a larger international campaign to put pressure on the government of South Africa to eliminate the practice of apartheid.

Cricket's Return to the International Stage

The eventual readmission of South Africa to international cricket served as a watershed moment in the transformation of the country. It was the event that signaled the end of apartheid and the beginning of a new era in the history of South Africa.

The Rugby World Cup in 1995 and Nelson Mandela:

Nelson Mandela, the first democratically elected president of South Africa, used athletics as a unifying force to bring the country together. His involvement in the 1995 Rugby World Cup, which was portrayed in the movie "Invictus," served as a strong illustration of how sports can bring people together and promote a sense of national togetherness.

Cricket is Played in Dangerous Areas

Additionally, cricket has been used as a tool for diplomacy in areas that have been plagued by conflict and instability. The sport has been essential in bringing communities closer together and offering brief reprieves from the pressures of everyday life.

Afghanistan's national pastime, cricket:

The sport of cricket has made tremendous advances in Afghanistan, giving a source of national pride and unity in a country that has been defined by conflict.

The Afghan national cricket team's meteoric rise to prominence is a shining example of the transformative potential of competition in the face of adversity.

The sport of cricket in Kashmir:

Cricket has provided a momentary respite from the turbulence that has persisted for a long time in Kashmir, which has been a combat zone. People in the area have been able to put their differences aside, get together, and celebrate the sport thanks to the matches and tournaments that have taken place in the region.

In the modern day, cricket and diplomacy go hand in hand

In today's world, cricket continues to play an important role as a platform for fostering diplomatic relations and mediating disputes. Recent events provide evidence of its ongoing capacity to bring people together and encourage dialogue.

The role of cricket in Afghanistan's diplomatic efforts:

Afghanistan's diplomatic efforts have been helped along by the sport of cricket. The achievements of the Afghan cricket team on the international stage have given the country reason to be proud and have paved the way for improvements in the country's diplomatic and international ties.

The Influence of the Indian Premier League (IPL) on Indian Cricket:

Players from all around the world have come together to compete in the Indian Premier League (IPL), which is one of the most prominent cricket leagues in the world. This international league exemplifies how the bond of athletics can extend beyond the confines of a nation and cultivate brotherhood among players hailing from a variety of cultural and ethnic backgrounds.

Cricket as a Means of Exerting Soft Power:

Cricket has been utilized as an effective instrument of soft power by countries such as India. They have increased their diplomatic ties and expanded their worldwide influence by engaging with cricket-playing nations and staging international competitions.

The fact that cricket has been used as a tool for diplomacy and the resolution of conflicts is evidence of the extraordinary power of the sport to bring people together, overcome divisions, and go beyond the constraints of political and cultural norms. Cricket has shown that it has the potential to build diplomacy and bring nations together, as evidenced by its role in the campaign against apartheid in South Africa and the cricket rivalry between India and Pakistan.

The spirit of cricket continues to give opportunities for communication and hope in a world that is marked by geopolitical tensions and conflicts. The competition serves as a timely reminder that perseverance and solidarity in the face of adversity may be achieved via the pursuit of shared interests and objectives. The diplomatic power of cricket is as strong as it has ever been, and its influence will continue to mold international relations and encourage relationships between nations for many years to come.

8.1 Cricket as a diplomatic tool in international relations

Cricket, also known as the "gentleman's game," has a long history of playing a special role in the process of international diplomacy. This has been the case for a number of years. Even though cricket is generally played as a sport, it has on numerous occasions crossed over into the realm of diplomacy and has been used to facilitate better international relations. Because of cricket's widespread popularity, as well as its long and illustrious history and devoted following, the sport has been instrumental in fostering diplomatic relations and bringing together nations. In this essay of 2000 words, we will discuss how cricket has been used as a kind of diplomacy in the context of international relations. We shall investigate its historical background as well as its relevance in the present day for the purposes of encouraging peace, advancing diplomatic relations, and fortifying international links.

The Use of Cricket as an Instrument of Soft Power

The effect of cricket extends beyond the confines of the cricket field. It has become a kind of soft power, which is a non-coercive approach to international affairs that makes use of a nation's culture, values, and traditions in order to exercise influence and improve its place in the world. Cricket is a powerful instrument of soft power for nations in which the sport is popular due to its large following, rich traditions, and the emotional connection it forms with fans. This connection is formed due to the emotional connection it forms with fans.

Contextualization of the Past

Beginning with cricket's infancy comes the sport's long and illustrious tradition of playing an important part in international relations. As a result of the growth of the British Empire in the 19th century, the sport of cricket was taken to many new locations across the world. As a result of the legacy left by the British Empire, cricket became an important component of the cultural and social fabric of a large number of the countries that were a part of that empire. As a result of these countries gaining their independence, cricket evolved into a symbol of national pride as well as a platform for political expression.

During its fight for independence, India, for instance, utilized cricket as a means of asserting its identity and expressing its aspirations.

The sport offered a stage for indigenous people to demonstrate their skills, engage in head-to-head competition with their colonial overlords, and garner renown on a global scale. The early usage of cricket in India's fight for independence helped lay the groundwork for the sport's future use as a diplomatic tool for the country.

India and Pakistan Engaged in Some Diplomatic Cricket Action

One of the most notable examples of cricket's use as a diplomatic instrument is the intense rivalry that exists between India and Pakistan in the game of cricket. The competition between these two adjacent countries, which has been marked by tensions both historically and politically, has frequently been soothed by the sport of cricket.

The Game of Cricket During Times of War:

Even during periods of heightened political animosity between the two countries, India and Pakistan have continued to compete against each other in cricket matches. Both countries can demonstrate a more cordial aspect of their relationship by competing against one another on the cricket field, which is an objective environment that is free from bias.

Cricket Matches as Opportunities for Bilateral Cooperation:

The bilateral endeavors of India and Pakistan to enhance their diplomatic relations have occasionally taken the form of cricket matches between the two countries. Both nations' top officials have been seen cheering on their teams at high-profile matches, where they have had the chance to engage in casual conversation with one another.

Diplomacy with the Public:

The competition between India and Pakistan in cricket has also been used as a method of public diplomacy. It enables people from both countries to communicate with one another and participate in a hobby or interest they have in common, which helps to cultivate human relationships and people-to-people ties.

Cricket as a Force for Harmony:

Cricket tournaments dubbed "Cricket for Peace" are only one example of the initiatives that have been launched to foster peace and understanding between India and Pakistan. Cricket is used as a vehicle by these projects to bring people together and highlight the similarities that exist across the various cultures involved.

The Effect that Participation in International Tournaments Have

The ICC Cricket World Cup and the ICC Twenty20 World Cup are two examples of international cricket competitions that serve as a stage for the advancement of diplomatic efforts and the fortification of international relations. The ability of sport to bring people together across cultural and political divides is demonstrated by the fact that many different types of teams compete in these competitions.

Diplomacy during the Cricket World Cup:

One noteworthy illustration of how cricket can help to facilitate diplomatic relations is provided

by the Cricket World Cup. Whether they choose to host or participate in the event, nations are brought together, and their leaders have the opportunity to engage in diplomatic conversations.

Cricket and the Politics of Bilateral Ties:

There are many possibilities for countries to cultivate or deepen their diplomatic relationships

with other nations that play cricket at the international level during international competitions. They offer a venue for influential people to get together and talk about a variety of topics while appreciating the sport.

Connecting Individuals with One Another:

Fans from all around the world come together to cheer on their national teams during

international competitions, which fosters the development of new personal relationships. These encounters can lead to the exchange of cultural traditions and a greater comprehension of the people and customs of other nations.

In the modern day, cricket and diplomacy go hand in hand

In today's globe, cricket continues to play an important role as a diplomatic tool, which exemplifies the sport's persistent capacity to bring people together and encourage conversation.

The role of cricket in Afghanistan's diplomatic efforts:

In a country that is plagued by conflict, the cricket team of Afghanistan has made great international accomplishments, bringing a sense of solidarity and pride to the people of Afghanistan. Because of the achievements of the Afghan national soccer team, new channels for diplomacy and international relations have been opened, and Afghanistan is now able to communicate with the rest of the world by means of sports.

The Influence of the Indian Premier League (IPL) on Indian Cricket:

Players hailing from a variety of nationalities and backgrounds compete in the Indian Premier League, which is consistently ranked as one of the most popular cricket tournaments on a global scale. The global aspect of the Indian Premier League demonstrates how sports can cross national boundaries and how it may develop brotherhood among players from a variety of cultural backgrounds.

Cricket as a Means of Exerting Soft Power:

The sport of cricket has been skillfully employed as a kind of soft power by countries such as India. They have increased their diplomatic ties and expanded their worldwide influence by engaging with cricket-playing nations and staging international competitions.

The Practice of Diplomacy in the Twenty-First Century

In the twenty-first century, cricket has continued to be an important factor in the development of

diplomacy and other aspects of international relations. Regardless of the political or ideological differences that exist between them, it provides nations with a shared ground on which they can hold conversations and construct bridges.

Cricket's function as a diplomatic weapon in international relations is a tribute to its unique capacity to connect people, bridge divides, and transcend political and cultural boundaries. This ability has allowed cricket to play an important part in international politics. Cricket has demonstrated how shared passions and similar goals can triumph over even the most difficult of conditions, and it has done so in a variety of contexts, including the cricket competition between India and Pakistan and the fight against apartheid in South Africa.

The spirit of cricket continues to give opportunities for communication and hope in a world that is marked by geopolitical tensions and conflicts. The game acts as a reminder that a nation's culture, heritage, and common values may bring people from other countries together, so fostering peace and diplomacy and forging bonds that will last. The diplomatic power of cricket is as strong as it has ever been, and its influence will continue to shape international relations and strengthen connections between states for a great many years to come.

8.2 High-profile series and their geopolitical significance

Cricket, a sport that is loved and admired in many regions of the world, has frequently grown into a function that is more significant than that of a simple kind of amusement. Both in the past and in the present, high-profile cricket series have played a key role in the international political landscape. This article of 1000 words dives into the geopolitical relevance of such series, analyzing how they have played a role in forming international relations, promoting diplomacy, and influencing public perceptions.

The study focuses on the role that such series have played in shaping international relations, promoting diplomacy, and influencing public perceptions.

Before we begin:

Cricket has repeatedly demonstrated that it is much more than just a sport; rather, it is a cultural phenomenon that incites passion and devotion among its millions of devoted followers. The Ashes, conflicts between India and Pakistan, and the Border-Gavaskar Trophy are all examples of high-profile cricket series that extend beyond the confines of the playing field. The geopolitical and socioeconomic processes that characterize our planet are reflected in these series like a mirror. They demonstrate the long-standing rivalries, the drive for domination, and the potential for achieving diplomatic goals through the medium of sport. This essay will investigate the impact of these high-profile cricket series from a geopolitical perspective, focusing on how they affect both international relations and popular image.

Contextualization of the Past

It is vital to conduct research into the historical context of high-profile cricket series if one wishes to comprehend the geopolitical significance of these matches. The origins of several of these series may be traced back at least a century, and they were frequently conceived during periods of tense political climate and colonial rule. Let's look at a couple of these historical series together.

What Remains:

The first match of the Ashes series, which pitted England's cricket team against Australia's, took place in 1882–1883. It is important from a geopolitical standpoint because of the intense sporting competition that exists between the two countries, with the series acting as a metaphor for a war for cricketing supremacy. Since England's loss to Australia, the cricket trophy known as the "Ashes" has evolved into a symbol of both national pride and competitiveness between the two countries.

Pakistan and India:

India and Pakistan have been rivals in the sport of cricket since its inception in 1952, not long after the two countries achieved their independence from British domination. In the difficult relationship that exists between the two countries, it has functioned as a diplomatic tool by providing a platform for engagement and relation-ships between individuals of both nations.

The Border-Gavaskar Trophy consists of:

Both India and Australia compete for the Border-Gavaskar Trophy, which was named after two of the most illustrious players in the history of cricket: Allan Border and Sunil Gavaskar. The series, which has been played since 1996, is a reflection of the larger geopolitical significance of the relationship between India and Australia as well as their prominence in the world of cricket.

Importance from a Geopolitical Perspective

Patriotism and a Sense of National Identity:

These competitions frequently serve as a sign of national pride and identity for the nations that take part in them. The Ashes, for instance, is more than just a cricket series; it is a manifestation of the long-standing competition that has existed between England and Australia.

Diplomacy and Methods of Resolving Conflict:

Cricket provides a forum for the practice of diplomacy and the resolution of disputes. In spite of the political tensions between India and Pakistan, diplomacy and links between the two countries' populations have been fostered through activities such as cricket matches between the two countries.

Relations with Other Countries:

These series help to improve international relations by bringing people from different countries together and promoting a sense of solidarity among spectators and players. For example, the Border-Gavaskar Trophy is symbolic of the relationship that exists between India and Australia in the context of the larger picture of world politics.

The Ashes: A Symbol of Supremacy in Sporting Competition

The Ashes series that is being played between England and Australia is of major importance in geopolitical terms. Not only does it signify a conflict between two sports teams, but it also symbolizes a struggle for dominance and an ongoing contest throughout history.

A Symbol of Pride for the Nation:

Both England and Australia consider winning the Ashes to be a source of national pride and identity. It is a matter of immense prestige to win the Ashes series since it indicates superiority in the sport that was originally forced on the colonies by the British Empire. Cricket is played in the colonies.

Beyond the Boundaries of Sport:

The competition for the Ashes between England and Australia extends well beyond the sport of cricket. It shapes the perceptions and ideas of people about the relative strengths of the two states, which in turn influences the discourse on international affairs.

Public Opinion and the Promotion of National Unity:

Both countries' popular mood is significantly affected by the outcome of the Ashes series. A victory in the series has the potential to strengthen national unity and act as a rallying point for the country's population.

Importance in the Present Day and Age

Cricket tournaments with a high profile continue to have an impact on the state of international relations in the modern world. The geopolitics of cricket have developed in tandem with the shifting landscape of the global political landscape.

The Expanding Scope of India's Impact:

The increasing geopolitical influence of India has been reflected by the country's meteoric rise in international cricket. The Indian Premier League, or IPL, is one of the most lucrative cricket tournaments and serves as a showcase for India's soft power as well as its economic might.

Sport as a Tool for International Diplomacy:

The International Cricket Council (ICC) Cricket World Cup is one example of an international cricket competition that serves as a forum for international diplomacy. The ability to participate in diplomatic conversations and to fortify relationships is afforded to nations who either host or take part in these tournaments.

The Exchange of Cultures:

Cricket encourages the sharing of culture between different countries. Leagues and international competitions bring together players from a wide variety of ethnic backgrounds, which promotes contact and understanding amongst people of different cultures.

The geopolitical impact of high-profile cricket series goes much beyond the confines of the cricket field itself. They are used as a symbol of national pride and identity, as a tool for facilitating diplomacy and the resolution of conflicts, and as a means of influencing international relations and public opinion.

These series offer a glimpse into the intricate interplay between geopolitics and sports, ranging from the long-standing competition over the Ashes to the important diplomatic role played by cricket matches between India and Pakistan. In today's world, cricket continues to play an important role in international diplomacy because of its ability to inspire goodwill, encourage cooperation, and promote harmony. Through the medium of sport, these series will continue to affect international relations and contribute to the rich fabric of global diplomacy as they continue to develop.

8.3 The power of cricket in fostering international cooperation

Cricket, also known as the "gentleman's game," is not only a pastime but also a potent force for developing international collaboration. The sport was first played in India in the 18th century. This essay of 1000 words examines how cricket transcends borders, establishes bridges between nations, and acts as a vehicle for diplomacy and world solidarity. Specifically, it looks at how cricket has been used in the Indian subcontinent.

Before we begin:

The sport of cricket, which has a long and illustrious history and is played all over the world,

possesses a special power that can unite both individuals and entire nations. In addition to being a means for international cooperation, it is a sport that brings fans together in an expression of delight and excitement for the game. The sport of cricket is beneficial to international relations because it bridges political and cultural divides and encourages solidarity among nations. In this essay, we will look into the power of cricket in fostering international collaboration and explore its impact on diplomacy, public perception, and cultural exchange. In addition, we will investigate the power of cricket in fostering international cooperation.

The Game of Cricket Is a Global Language

One of cricket's most powerful qualities in promoting international collaboration is its ability to appeal to people all over the world. It is played, observed, and revered in a wide variety of cultures, linguistic communities, and geographic areas. Because of its widespread popularity, cricket has become a universal language that fans of all walks of life can relate to, understand, and appreciate.

A Driving Force Towards Unity:

For example, the International Cricket Council (ICC) Cricket World Cup brings together teams from a wide variety of countries, displaying the rich diversity that exists throughout the cricketing world. This competition serves as a worldwide celebration of the sport, bridging national barriers and bringing together enthusiasts from all over the world.

A Forum for the Exchange of Cultural Perspectives:

Cultural interaction is encouraged through participation in international cricket competitions. In the spirit of competitiveness, players from a variety of countries, each of which is steeped in its own distinctive traditions, come together. This connection between people of different cultures cultivates mutual respect and understanding.

Engagement of Fans Around the World:

The global fan base of cricket is very engaged in the sport and frequently transcends political,

ethnic, or religious ties in their participation. Cricket fan clubs, online discussion groups, and social media sites all serve as venues where individuals from a wide range of backgrounds may gather to discuss and enjoy the sport.

Relations between India and Pakistan, as Determined by Cricket Diplomacy

The intense competition between India and Pakistan in cricket provides one of the clearest illustrations of the positive role that cricket may play in promoting international cooperation. Both of these countries, who are neighbors and have a history of political conflicts, have frequently used cricket as a form of interaction and discussion between them.

Initiatives Regarding Diplomacy:

Cricket matches have been used as a form of diplomatic communication between India and Pakistan. The presidents of both countries have been able to participate in confidence-building measures by attending high-profile matches and having informal conversations with one another.

Diplomacy with the Public:

The cricket competition between India and Pakistan acts as a type of public diplomacy since it enables the people of both countries to communicate with one another and participate in an activity that they are passionate about. This helps to personalize the opposing viewpoint and establish ties between individual people.

Relations Between Two Countries:

Cricket has helped to improve relations between the two countries, which is a positive

development for both. Even during times of heightened political tension, matches and tournaments have provided opportunity for communication and contact between competing parties.

The diplomatic role of cricket in Afghanistan

Cricket has also been a crucial factor in Afghanistan's efforts to establish international collaboration in recent years. In a country that is plagued by conflict, the achievements of the Afghan national cricket team on the world stage have served as a source of national pride and solidarity.

Characterizing a Nation:

The ascent to prominence of the Afghan cricket team has evolved into a symbol of national identity and has become a unifying force for the country. It provides a sense of pride and success, as well as a good narrative for a society that is working toward peace and security.

Engagement with the World:

Afghanistan has been given the opportunity to interact with the international community as a result of the cricketing community's warm reception of the country. Afghanistan now has more opportunity to connect with other nations and demonstrate its capabilities on the international scene thanks to the sport of cricket.

Initiatives Regarding Diplomacy:

Cricket has been utilized by Afghanistan as a diplomatic instrument in order to create relationships with other countries. Cricket matches have opened up opportunities for diplomatic contacts and conversations, which has enabled the nation to develop its ties with other countries.

The Role of International Cricket Competitions in the Diplomatic Process

Tournaments of cricket played on a global scale, such as the Cricket World Cup hosted by the International Cricket Council (ICC), are an essential component in the process of building global cooperation. These competitions serve as a forum for diplomatic exchange by bringing different nations together and giving their leaders the opportunity to hold discussions on diplomatic matters.

Diplomacy during the Cricket World Cup:

The Cricket World Cup, the most important tournament in the history of the sport, is more than just a contest. It is a chance to improve diplomatic relations. The ability to create or strengthen diplomatic contacts with other nations who play cricket is a benefit that comes with either hosting or participating in the tournament.

Connecting Individuals with One Another:

People from all over the world come together to compete in international cricket events. As a result of supporting their own teams together, sports fans from all over the world are able to broaden their understanding of other countries and participate in cultural exchanges.

The Characteristics of a Good Sportsman:

The values of sportsmanship and fair play are emphasized heavily throughout cricket

competitions. This shared philosophy encourages the promotion of ideals that extend beyond the confines of the cricket pitch and has an impact on the way in which nations interact with one another.

The sport of cricket and international relations

Cricket has frequently contributed to the formation of international relations and diplomacy on a worldwide scale. It offers nations a common ground on which they can interact, communicate, and have conversations with one another.

Power and Influence through Soft Means

Cricket is an example of soft power, which refers to a non-confrontational approach to the conduct of international relations. It gives nations the opportunity to showcase their culture, values, and traditions on a worldwide scale, which enables them to influence public perception and build up good connotations.

Diplomacy via Economic Means:

High-profile cricket competitions, particularly leagues such as the Indian Premier League (IPL), have a considerable effect on the local and national economies. This economic influence can serve as a negotiating point in international relations, which opens the door to prospects for economic diplomacy.

Diplomacy through the Arts:

Cricket is beneficial to cultural diplomacy since players and supporters from different countries engage in cultural and traditional exchanges with one another while playing the game. The sharing of one's culture with members of other countries leads to a greater understanding and admiration of those countries.

It cannot be denied that cricket may be a powerful tool in the promotion of international cooperation. It functions as a universal language that bridges the gaps between different cultures, countries, and political systems.

The cricket competition between India and Pakistan is a great example of how cricket can help bring people from different countries closer together while also fostering diplomacy and ties between individuals.

Tournaments of international cricket provide opportunities for cultural and diplomatic interchange, thereby fostering a more sportsmanlike and level-headed attitude among competitors. Cricket is a tool of soft power that enables governments to influence public perception and generate good connections on a worldwide scale. This is made possible since cricket is played internationally.

Cricket's capacity to bring people from different countries together and to encourage

international collaboration is unrivaled in a world where geopolitical tensions and conflicts are on the rise. This serves as a reminder that the world may be brought together by shared passions, common ideals, and a commitment to fair play, all of which can foster peace, unity, and diplomacy. Cricket is more than simply a sport; it is a vehicle for global collaboration and understanding that continues to be shaped by the diplomatic power of cricket, which continues to affect international relations.

Chapter 9

Challenges and Controversies

Cricket, sometimes known as the "gentleman's game," has a long and illustrious history and is played by a significant number of people all over the world. Cricket, however, is not immune to the issues and controversies that face other sports, just like any other sport. Throughout its history, the sport has been confronted with a wide variety of challenges, including governance problems, instances of corruption, on-field confrontations, and ethical conundrums. In this essay of 3000 words, we will delve into the difficulties and controversies that have marred cricket's path, both historically and in the modern period. We will look at these issues from both perspectives: the past and the present. We are going to investigate the impact that these problems have had on the game and the people who have a stake in it, as well as the steps that have been made to remedy these problems.

Historically Significant Difficulties and Debates
The Bodyline Series, which ran from 1932 to 1933:
The Bodyline series was one of the earliest disputes to arise in the sport of cricket. It took place during the Ashes series, which was played between England and Australia. As a result of England's aggressive strategies, which included bowlers aiming at the body of the Australian batters, diplomatic tensions arose, and discussions on the ethical implications of the sport were held.

The D'Oliveira Affair (which took place in 1968):
An international incident occurred when the cricket player Basil D'Oliveira, who is of mixed race and was born in South Africa, was chosen to play for England in a match versus South Africa. The apartheid government of South Africa raised objections to D'Oliveira's participation, which led to the postponement of the tour and further isolated South African cricket from the rest of the world cricket community.

1981: The Year of the "Underarm Bowling Incident"
During a One-Day International match between Australia and New Zealand, the Australian team used a controversial strategy by delivering the final ball of the match with an underarm delivery. This prevented New Zealand from scoring the required

runs and won the match for Australia. This incident aroused controversy, which ultimately led to revisions in the rules and regulations that govern cricket.

Contemporary Issues That Are Creating Controversy

Corruption and the fixing of matches:

Corruption and the fixing of matches has emerged as one of the most critical concerns facing modern cricket. The sport's legitimacy and reputation have taken a hit as a result of a number of high-profile scandals involving players, officials, and bookies. Cricket's governing bodies and boards have taken action to tackle this problem, including the establishment of anti-corruption sections and the implementation of stringent rules of conduct.

The Match-Fixing Scandal that Engulfed the Indian Premier League (IPL) in 2013:

When players and team officials were found to have been involved in illicit betting and spot-fixing, the Indian Premier League (IPL), which is one of the most popular cricket leagues, was rocked by a major controversy. The incident caused people to question the integrity of the league's governance, which ultimately led to changes being made to the league's administration.

Player Conduct and Controversies that Occur on the Field:

Sledging, dissension, and physical altercations are just some of the examples of poor player behavior that have occurred on the cricket field in recent years. These kinds of instances might leave a negative impression of the game and call for the intervention of the regulatory organizations in order to preserve order.

The Decision Review System, also abbreviated as DRS:

The debut of the DRS in cricket has caused discussions and controversies, mainly over the reliability of the technology, the fairness of the system, and the choices made by the umpires. Various stakeholders each have their own unique perspective regarding the effect that the DRS has on the game.

Ethical Challenges Facing the Sport of Cricket

Responsibilities of Players and Expectations Placed Upon Them

It is common for spectators to look up to cricket players as role models, both on and off the field.

When the acts of players, whether they pertain to the player's personal conduct, substance addiction, or on-field behavior, do not line with these expectations, an ethical dilemma might result.

Tampering with the Ball Scandals:

Incidents of ball-tampering, such as the infamous "Sandpaper Gate" that occurred in 2018 involving the Australian cricket team, push the sport's ethical bounds to their limits. These kinds of acts not only have repercussions for the individuals who were engaged, but they also call into question what we mean when we talk about the "spirit of cricket."

Ethical Concerns Regarding the Health of Players:

The current game of cricket places a premium on high levels of performance, which can often give rise to ethical considerations regarding the health and wellbeing of players. The ethics of pushing athletes to their limits have been called into question due to concerns over burnout, mental health, and physical weariness among other factors.

Problems to Be Encountered in Both Governance and Administration

Failure of Cricket Boards to Maintain Transparency:

Several cricket boards and regulatory bodies have come under fire for their apparent bias, lack of openness, and opaque decision-making processes. Because of this, there have been calls for increased accountability as well as improvements to governance.

Potentially Conflicting Interests:

Individuals who have various responsibilities, such as being team owners, commentators, or selectors while simultaneously serving in administrative posts have caused problems with conflict of interest in cricket administration. Concerns regarding the fairness of decision-making are raised when such conflicts occur.

Disproportionate Sharing of the Wealth:

The financial structure of international cricket has come under fire for being perceived as unfairly tilted in favor of the main cricketing nations, which puts smaller and associate member states at a financial disadvantage. Because of this disparity, many have started talking about the need for a more equitable distribution of wealth.

The Repercussions of Market Orientation

The commercial pressure that players are under:

The increasing commercialization of cricket has resulted in a greater amount of pressure being placed on players to perform well, live up to the expectations of their sponsors, and maintain a positive public image. The mental and emotional health of athletes may suffer as a result of the stress they face.

The Increasing Number of Twenty20 Leagues:

Concerns have been made concerning the impact that Twenty20 leagues, such as the Indian Premier League (IPL), are having on the availability of players for international matches and more conventional forms of the game, despite the fact that these leagues have helped to popularize the sport and brought in a large amount of income.

An Excessive Dependence on Income from Broadcasting:

For cricket's long-term financial health, the cash produced from broadcasting rights has evolved into an increasingly important factor. However, due to its dependence on broadcast money, the scheduling of matches and the proper distribution of games between domestic and international competitions are sometimes subject to disruption.

Actions Taken in Response to Difficulties and Issues of Controversy

Units Dedicated to Combating Corruption

Anti-corruption units have been established by the governing bodies of cricket in order to monitor and prevent match-fixing as well as corruption. In order to investigate crimes and bring those responsible to justice, these groups work closely with law enforcement agencies.

Committees for Ethical Conduct:

Committees on ethics have been established by cricket governing bodies in order to address concerns regarding player conduct, ethical conundrums, and conflicts of interest. The purpose of these committees is to make certain that the game is played honestly and in accordance with its fundamental principles.

Regulations Regarding the Code of Conduct and Punishment:

In order to maintain order both on and off the field of play, cricket governing bodies have established codes of conduct and regulations for disciplinary action.

Everyone involved in the game, including players, referees, and support staff, is required to abide by these principles, and any violations will result in sanctions.

Reforms to the Governance:

Several cricket boards and governing bodies have implemented governance reforms in recent years with the goals of boosting transparency, decreasing the number of conflicts of interest, and guaranteeing a more equitable distribution of resources.

Programs for the Wellbeing of the Players:

Concerns about the welfare of cricket players have led some cricket governing bodies to implement player welfare programs. These programs address a variety of issues, including burnout, mental health, and substance addiction. These programs offer assistance and resources to help athletes maintain a healthy mental and physical state.

Cricket is not an exception to the rule that contests and debates are a natural and unavoidable component of every sport. Cricket has had its fair share of problems throughout its history, from age-old controversies like as the Bodyline to more recent problems such as corruption and ethics in the game. However, the sport's tenacity and commitment to upholding its integrity and principles is demonstrated by its ability to resolve these issues and conflicts.

The governing bodies of cricket have implemented a variety of reforms in recent years in order to eliminate corruption, improve governance, and maintain player discipline. Even in the face of challenges, the sport of cricket will continue to thrive and serve as an inspiration to succeeding generations thanks to their efforts, the fervor with which cricket fans follow the game, and the sport's ongoing popularity. Cricket is a sport that benefits from having obstacles and controversies, rather than suffering from them, because they make the sport more dynamic and entertaining.

9.1 Match-fixing and corruption

In recent decades, the "gentleman's game," cricket, has been overshadowed by the specter of match-fixing and corruption. Cricket is commonly referred to as the "gentleman's game." The sport, which has a devoted fan base all around the world, has been rocked by high-profile scandals in recent years, which have called into question its credibility and shaken its roots. In this article of 1500 words, we will dig into the murky realm of match-fixing and corruption in cricket. This is a sport with a long and storied history. We are going to look at the historical context, the influence on the game, the steps that have been done to tackle these challenges, as well as the ethical conundrums that they present.

Contextualization of the Past

Cricket has a long history marred by scandals involving match-fixing and other forms of misconduct. Instances of players trying to get an unfair advantage by manipulating the game extend back several decades, despite the fact that their methods have become increasingly complex and extensive over the years.

Instances of Match-Fixing in its Infancy:

It has been alleged that matches in the sport of cricket have been fixed as far back as the late 19th century. These early occurrences, which were frequently tied to illegal betting and had far-reaching repercussions for the sport's legitimacy, occurred when the sport was still in its infancy.

In the 1970s, Kerry Packer hosted the World Series Cricket:

In the 1970s, Kerry Packer introduced his World Series Cricket, which added a new facet to the sport's increasingly lucrative commercialization. Although it was not match-fixing in the conventional sense, it did mark a dramatic shift in the financial environment of the sport and had substantial ramifications for the regulation of the game.

Corruption in the 21st Century and Fixing of Matches:

Shockwaves were sent across the cricketing globe as a result of an increase in the number of match-fixing and corruption scandals that broke in the latter part of the 20th century and at the turn of the 21st century.

The Scandal Involving Hansie Cronje (2000):

The cricketing world was thrown into disarray when it was revealed that South African captain Hansie Cronje had been involved in a match-fixing controversy. Cronje's role in manipulating results, fixing matches, and accepting money from bookies brought to light the pervasiveness of bribery and other forms of corruption in the game.

A Scandal Involving the Fixing of Spots in Pakistan (2010):

Pakistani cricketers Salman Butt, Mohammad Amir, and Mohammad Asif were found guilty of spot-fixing during a test match played against England. Spot-fixing is a form of match-fixing in which some occurrences within a match are modified for the purposes of betting. This incident brought forth judicial proceedings, which in turn harmed Pakistan's reputation.

The scandals that occurred during the 2013 and 2015 seasons of the Indian Premier League (IPL):

Allegations of match-fixing and illicit betting were leveled against the Indian Premier League (IPL), one of the most lucrative Twenty20 tournaments. The involvement of high-profile players, team owners, and officials has brought into doubt the governance of the league as well as its commitment to upholding its integrity.

The Influence That It Had On the Game

Match-fixing and corruption have had significant repercussions for the sport of cricket, including negative effects on the sport's integrity, the public's opinion of it, and its capacity to remain financially viable.

Contamination of Integrity:

The scandals involving match-fixing and corruption have done significant damage to the sport of cricket's reputation for fair play. The image of the sport as a "gentleman's game" has been damaged, and fans, players, and authorities have all developed a pessimistic outlook on it.

The Opinions of the Public:

These scandals have had a huge impact on how the general public views cricket. There is a risk that spectators may lose faith in the genuineness of the competitions, and there is also a risk that sponsors and broadcasters will reconsider their financial commitments to the sport.

The Implications for Finance:

Scandals involving match-fixing can have serious ramifications for cricket's finances. There is a possibility that sponsorship deals, broadcasting rights, and ticket sales could be negatively impacted, which may have an effect on the game's long-term viability.

Efforts Made to Combat Fixing of Matches and Corruption in the Sport

In an effort to prevent match-fixing and corruption and to restore the sport's honor, the governing bodies of cricket and the stakeholders in the sport have instituted a number of reforms.

Units Dedicated to Combating Corruption

Governing bodies of cricket, such as the International Cricket Council (ICC), have created specialized anti-corruption sections in order to monitor and investigate instances of corrupt activity. In order to bring criminals to justice, these teams collaborate closely with law enforcement organizations.

Regulations Regarding Codes of Conduct and Other Disciplinary Matters:

In order to maintain discipline both on and off the field, various codes of conduct and regulations regarding disciplinary action have been put into place. Everyone involved in the game, including players, referees, and support staff, is required to abide by these principles, and any violations will result in sanctions.

Programs for People Who Whistleblower:

Programs designed to encourage persons who have information about corrupt activities to come forward and disclose that information have been put into place. Informants are afforded anonymity and protection through the use of these systems.

Education and a Consciousness of the Facts:

Education is provided to both the players and the officials of the perils of match-fixing and corruption. It is essential for people to have this understanding in order to reduce the likelihood that they may participate in unethical behaviors.

Committees for Ethical Conduct:

Committees on ethics have been established by cricket's governing bodies in order to handle issues with player conduct, ethical conundrums, and conflicts of interest. The purpose of these committees is to make certain that the game is played honestly and in accordance with its fundamental principles.

Ethical Challenges Facing the Sport of Cricket

The rigging of matches and other forms of corruption in cricket present a number of difficult moral questions and put the sport's core ideals and the obligations of its various stakeholders under scrutiny.

Responsibilities of Players and Expectations Placed Upon Them

On the field as well as off it, cricket players are frequently held up as examples to follow. When the acts of players, whether they pertain to the player's personal conduct, substance addiction, or on-field behavior, do not line with these expectations, an ethical dilemma might result.

Ethical Concerns Regarding the Health of Players:

In today's game of cricket, the pressure to perform at the greatest level possible raises ethical questions about the well-being and health of the players. The ethics of pushing athletes to their limits have been called into question due to concerns over burnout, mental health, and physical weariness among other factors.

Introducing the "Spirit of Cricket" :

The "spirit of cricket" is an important aspect of the game that places an emphasis on sportsmanship, fair play, and respect for one's competitors. This ethos is put to the test by match-fixing and corruption, which also creates ethical tensions for the players and authorities involved.

Concerns Relating to Openness and Good Governance

Failure of Cricket Boards to Maintain Transparency:

Several cricket boards and regulatory bodies have come under fire for their apparent bias, lack of openness, and opaque decision-making processes. Because of this, there have been calls for increased accountability as well as improvements to governance.

Potentially Conflicting Interests:

Individuals who have various responsibilities, such as being team owners, commentators, or selectors while simultaneously serving in administrative posts have caused problems with conflict of interest in cricket administration. Concerns regarding the fairness of decision-making are raised when such conflicts occur.

The influence of business on the players

An Excessive Dependence on Income from Broadcasting:

For cricket's long-term financial health, the cash produced from broadcasting rights has evolved into an increasingly important factor. However, due to its dependence on broadcast money, the scheduling of matches and the proper distribution of games between domestic and international competitions are sometimes subject to disruption.

Increasing Number of Twenty20 Leagues:

Concerns have been made concerning the impact that Twenty20 leagues, such as the Indian Premier League (IPL), are having on the availability of players for international matches and more conventional forms of the game, despite the fact that these leagues have helped to popularize the sport and brought in a large amount of income.

The Process of Commercializing the Game:

The commercialization of the sport has resulted in significant financial gains, but it has also given rise to ethical problems concerning the sport's values. Maintaining a healthy equilibrium between the demands of economic interests and the game's fundamental principles is an ongoing problem.

Integrity and credibility face enormous issues in the sport of cricket as a result of match-fixing and corruption. The gravity of the issue is shown by the historical background, recent scandals, and the effect those have had on the sport's reputation as well as its financial standing.

Anti-corruption units, codes of conduct, education programs, and whistleblower campaigns are some of the results of efforts to tackle these challenges that have led to the development of these entities. In addition, the game's ideals and principles are being monitored by ethics committees, and governance improvements are being implemented with this goal in mind.

The sport of cricket continues to struggle with difficult moral questions concerning the obligations of players, their health, and the "spirit of cricket." Ongoing obstacles include concerns around transparency as well as the increasing commercialization of the game.

Even while cricket has made some headway in combating match-fixing and other forms of corruption, the sport still needs to be on its guard in order to preserve its reputation as a worldwide favorite and a role model for good sportsmanship and competitive spirit. In order to maintain its status as an honorable and open sport in the face of these problems, cricket will need the concerted efforts of its regulatory bodies, players, officials, and fans.

9.2 Issues related to governance and administration

Cricket, a sport played and enjoyed by millions of people all over the world, is not without of difficulties, notably in the areas of governance and administration. Concerns and arguments centering on the management and administration of cricket have been the focus of a lot of attention and discussion in recent years. In this essay of 1000 words, we are going to discuss the governance and administrative difficulties that have been a problem for the sport. We are going to go into problems such as financial inequities, commercialization, conflicts of interest, and transparency, and we will emphasize the influence that these issues have on the game as well as potential remedies.

Before we begin:

Cricket is a sport that has been played for a long time and has a significant following all over the world. On the other hand, government and administration play a significant part in determining the course that the sport will take, just as they would in any undertaking of this magnitude. Concerns pertaining to these facets may have far-reaching ramifications, which may have an effect on the growth, integrity, and fairness of the sport. In this essay, we will investigate some of the key difficulties that exist within the governance and administration of cricket. We will look at how these challenges affect the game and what steps have been done to address them.

Lack of accountability and transparency in government operations

The absence of openness and accountability within cricket's regulatory bodies is one of the most significant obstacles that must be overcome in order to successfully administer the sport. This problem has an effect on the procedures used to make decisions, the administration of finances, and the public's trust in general.

Making Decisions in the Dark:

Many cricket boards and governing bodies have been criticized for making decisions in private, without involving important stakeholders or providing explanations for their decisions. This has led to criticism from the cricket community. This lack of openness can rise to questions about the validity of the decision-making process as well as concerns about whether or not it is fair.

The Appearance of Favoritism:

Some people have the impression that the administration of cricket is influenced by personal, political, or financial interests. This is also true in some circumstances. This view undermines public faith in the governing organizations, which in turn can lead to disillusionment on the part of supporters.

Accountability to the Public and Other Stakeholders:

The administration of cricket ought to be answerable to the general public, cricket's supporters and players, and any other stakeholders. It is imperative that decision-making processes, financial management, and governance structures be conducted in a transparent manner if the sport is to recover the public's trust and preserve its integrity.

Incompatibility of Interests

Individuals who occupy several responsibilities in the administration of cricket, as well as individuals who have personal interests that may affect their ability to make objective decisions, contribute significantly to the problem of conflict of interest.

Multiple Functions:

A great number of people involved in cricket administration, commentary, and even former

Players occupy several responsibilities within the sport, such as being owners of teams, selectors, or members of governing bodies. Because of these many roles, there is a possibility that a player's personal interests will come into direct competition with those of the team.

Independence from Influence and Decision-Making:

Instances where there is a conflict of interest might give rise to questions regarding the impartiality of decision-makers. Fans and other stakeholders are concerned that personal or commercial interests may be taking precedence over the health of the sport when choices are being made.

Codes of conduct and other institutional changes:

Cricket's governing bodies and boards have instituted new codes of conduct and governance reforms in an effort to address concerns over potential conflicts of interest. These procedures intend to ensure that persons in positions of authority operate in a manner that is beneficial to the sport overall by requiring them to do so.

Disparities in Financial Resources

There is a significant income gap within the sport of cricket, with big cricketing nations receiving

more from the sport's revenues than smaller or associate member states, which have significant financial issues. This inequality has been a source of worry.

Inequality on a Financial Level:

The major cricketing nations, such as India, England, and Australia, have significant broadcasting and sponsorship deals, which result in substantial revenue for the respective countries. Smaller or associate member nations, on the other hand, receive a much smaller proportion of the total revenue generated by the sport.

Distribution Based on Fairness:

There have been cries for the sport of cricket to adopt a revenue distribution system that is more fair. The International Cricket Council (ICC) has responded to this issue by distributing cash to associate member nations as well as rising cricket nations. These efforts were done in an effort to address the problem.

Support for the Athletic Endeavor:

It is crucial to ensure financial parity in cricket if the sport is going to continue to grow and thrive in the future. Smaller nations are given the opportunity to improve their cricketing infrastructure and compete at the highest level when there is an equitable allocation of resources.

The Process of Commercializing the Game

The commercialization of cricket has resulted in a variety of positive outcomes, but it has also created a number of obstacles with regard to the fundamental principles and goals of the sport.

Keeping in Mind the Conflicting Commercial Interests:

There may be instances when the demands of economic interests, such as media deals and sponsorships, come into conflict with the traditional values of the sport as well as the well-being of the players. Finding a happy medium is of the utmost importance.

Influence on the Availability of Players:

Concerns have been raised over the availability of players for international matches as well as for the more conventional forms of the game as a result of the emergence of Twenty20 leagues such as the Indian Premier League (IPL). This issue has the potential to have repercussions for the level of play in international cricket.

Advancing the Core Values of the Sport:

The principles of cricket, including sportsmanship, fair play, and the "spirit of the game," should not be lost in the shuffle as the sport becomes increasingly commercialized. The continued upholding of these standards is absolutely necessary for the sport of cricket to thrive in the long run.

Attempts Made to Address Governance and Administrative Concerns through Various Measures

In the sport of cricket, there have been efforts made to address various governance and administrative difficulties. These steps are intended to improve financial parity, reduce the likelihood of conflicts of interest, increase transparency, and protect the core ideals of the sport.

Accountability and Openness to the Public:

The various boards and governing bodies of cricket have been pushed to adopt more transparency in the procedures that they use to make decisions. They have also been given the recommendation to involve important stakeholders, ensure public accountability, and provide transparent explanations for the actions that they have taken.

Regulations Regarding Potential Conflicts of Interest:

In order to address concerns regarding conflicts of interest, various governance reforms and codes of conduct have been put into place. These safeguards ensure that those in positions of authority are able to make judgments without being influenced by their own personal or financial interests.

Redistribution of Financial Resources:

The International Cricket Council (ICC) has begun implementing money redistribution plans to assist developing cricket nations and those with a smaller cricketing presence. The purpose of these initiatives is to guarantee that the aforementioned nations will receive sufficient funds for the improvement of their infrastructure and the marketing of their sport.

Keeping in Mind the Conflicting Commercial Interests:

The various boards and governing bodies of cricket are attempting to strike a balance between the sport's values and the business interests of the game. They have a responsibility to put the well-being of the players, the integrity of international cricket, and the advancement of the fundamental principles of the sport first.

Questions pertaining to cricket's governance and administration have been the focus of a significant amount of discussion and worry. There are a number of difficulties that need to be addressed in order to protect the sport's credibility and assure its further development. These challenges include commercialization, financial inequality, conflict of interest, and transparency and accountability.

There have been efforts made to improve the governance and administration of cricket through the implementation of measures such as transparency, codes of conduct, financial redistribution, and a strategy that is balanced toward commercialization. These programs have the goals of preserving the core values of the sport, advancing the cause of fair play, and ensuring that cricket will continue to prosper and serve as an inspiration to future generations.

Governance and administration in cricket are both crucial components that need to be in line with the fundamental tenets of the sport in order to protect cricket's unique identity and ensure that it continues to be a popular sport on a worldwide scale. If these difficulties are collaboratively addressed, it will be possible to guarantee that cricket will continue to be a sport that upholds integrity, transparency, and worldwide appeal.

9.3 The struggle for inclusion and diversity

The sport of cricket, which has a long and eventful history, has had its fair share of problems when it comes to fostering an inclusive and diverse environment. In spite of its widespread popularity, there have been considerable obstacles in the way of ensuring equal opportunities and representation for people hailing from a variety of different backgrounds. In this essay of 1000 words, we will investigate the fight for inclusion and diversity in cricket by looking at the historical barriers, the influence on the game, and the steps taken to resolve these challenges.

Before we begin:

Despite its widespread reputation as a sport that is accessible to players of all nationalities and cultural backgrounds, cricket has, over its long and illustrious existence, been forced to address challenges relating to diversity and inclusion. Cricket has had difficulty ensuring that all individuals have equal opportunity to join, contribute, and thrive in the sport due to racial disparities, gender biases, and socioeconomic inequalities, among other types of inequities. In this essay, we will investigate the historical context, current issues, and continuous fight for inclusion and diversity in cricket.

Barriers to Inclusion and Diversity That Have Persisted Throughout History

Segregation Based on Race:

During the time period of colonial rule, racial segregation practices were enforced in many nations, which reduced the number of options available to non-white communities to participate in cricket. For example, during the time of apartheid in South Africa, the country's cricket system was highly segregated, with white and non-white players competing in separate leagues and using separate facilities.

Disparities Between the Sexes:

Cricket has always been a male-dominated activity, and there are few opportunities for women to compete at a competitive level within the sport. Significant obstacles have been presented to women's participation in the game as a result of the cultural norms and expectations that surround gender roles.

Disparities in Socioeconomic Status:

The cost of playing cricket, which includes the cost of equipment, coaching, and access to facilities, has resulted in socioeconomic discrepancies in the number of people who participate in the sport. People who come from economically poor origins frequently encounter obstacles on their path to entrance.

Challenges Facing Inclusion and Diversity in the Modern World

Even if there have been advancements, the modern game of cricket is still struggling with problems that are associated with inclusion and diversity.

Disparities Between the Sexes:

There are still inequalities in terms of money, media attention, and possibilities for women who play cricket, despite the sport's substantial progress in this area. There is a considerable wage difference between male and female players in the sport of cricket, with male players often earning a lot more money than their female counterparts.

The Problem of Insufficient Representation of Minorities:

There are still problems in several countries that play cricket due to the under-representation of minority communities, notably in administrative and leadership positions. Because of this lack of variety, the sport may not be as welcoming to everyone.

Discrimination based on Race:

The image of the sport has been tainted by instances of racial prejudice both on and off the playing field. Sledging and verbal abuse are two examples of the kinds of racist behavior that continue to be a concern.

Obstacles of a Socioeconomic Nature:

It is possible for bright people who come from less privileged circumstances to be priced out of

playing competitive cricket due to the costs associated with the sport. These costs include coaching fees, equipment costs, and travel expenditures. Because of this, the sport's potential pool of talent is reduced.

Influence on the Course of Play

Cricket has been significantly altered as a result of the ongoing fight for more inclusivity and diversity in the sport.

Unrealized Potential:

When talented individuals from a variety of backgrounds are prevented from participating in a sport due to the existence of entry barriers, the sport suffers. This potential, which is now being underutilized, acts as a barrier to the progression of the sport at all levels.

Alternative points of view:

The richness of the sport is enhanced by both its inclusiveness and its diversity. Innovation and expansion are two outcomes that might result from incorporating a variety of perspectives into planning, training, and management.

Appeal to the World:

When different populations are represented in cricket, the game's popularity on a worldwide scale increases. A sport that welcomes more participants has the potential to grow in popularity over a wider range of geographic areas.

Activities Conducted in Order to Foster Inclusion and Diversity

The governing bodies of cricket and the stakeholders in the sport have each taken different steps to encourage inclusion and diversity.

The Development of Women's Cricket:

The expansion of women's cricket has resulted in a number of beneficial changes, including greater funding, the formation of new leagues, and the hosting of international championships. Women's cricket has received more attention as a result of competitions such as the ICC Women's World Cup and the Women's T20 World Cup.

Programs Fostering Diversity and Inclusion:

Numerous cricket boards have begun diversity and inclusion programs in order to pave the way for individuals who come from backgrounds that are under-represented in the sport. These programs intend to eliminate inequalities and make possibilities available to everyone.

Policies Regarding Discrimination Based on Race and Gender:

In order to combat problems of abuse and discrimination both on and off the field, stringent policies against racial and gender discrimination have been put into place. These policies have been put in place. Everyone involved in the game, including players, officials, and supporters, is expected to abide by these policies.

Community Action and Participation at the Local Level:

Community outreach and grassroots initiatives have been created by cricket boards in order to scout young talent from a variety of cultural and socioeconomic backgrounds at an early age and offer them with the resources and support necessary to excel in the sport.

The Approach Going Forward

The fight for inclusion and diversity in cricket is still continuing strong, and there is a great deal of work left to be done.

Equal Opportunities and Equal Compensation:

It is essential to work toward achieving pay parity and equal opportunity for male and female cricket players. In order for athletes of either gender to reach their full potential, they need access to the same resources, facilities, and support.

Regarding Representation in Positions of Leadership:

It is necessary to have a greater representation of persons from a variety of backgrounds in leadership roles within cricket, especially on boards and governing bodies.

This can be helpful in ensuring that the administration of the sport accurately represents the diverse player base of the sport.

Educational Programs and Activities:

The implementation of educational programs that promote anti-discrimination, diversity, and inclusion ought to be a top focus. These programs have the potential to build a culture of respect and inclusiveness at all levels of cricket, from the recreational to the professional level.

Initiatives to Combat Racism:

The sport of cricket ought to maintain its position at the forefront of anti-racism activities and efforts to eradicate racial discrimination inside the game. Combating racism requires a multifaceted approach that includes fostering diversity and inclusion.

The journey toward more inclusivity and diversity in cricket is one that is both difficult and continuing. The significance of this effort is highlighted by a number of factors, including the impact on the game, historical impediments, and modern challenges. Cricket's governing bodies and stakeholders have made progress in encouraging inclusion and diversity through a variety of programs and regulations, but there is still more to be done to ensure that cricket genuinely becomes a sport that anyone from any background may participate in, regardless of their gender, ethnicity, or origin.

Inclusion and diversity not only contribute to the enrichment of the sport, but also to its expansion and attractiveness across the world. As the game of cricket continues to develop, it is more important than ever to solve these concerns in order to maintain the sport's credibility, importance, and widespread appeal. The never-ending fight for inclusion and diversity is not merely a question of sportsmanship; rather, it is a manifestation of the ideals and tenets that cricket ought to uphold.

Chapter 10

Cricket's Future

The sport of cricket, which is frequently referred to as a "gentleman's game," has undergone substantial change over the years, shifting from a conventional sporting event to a global entertainment spectacle. Cricket, a sport that can trace its origins back to the 16th century, has seen numerous shifts in how it is played, how it is facilitated technologically, and how it is marketed to consumers. As we move forward into the future, cricket will be presented with a number of chances and challenges that will shape its terrain in ways that have never been seen before. This investigation digs at the future of cricket, focusing on its technological developments, commercial possibilities, and global expansion, as well as the repercussions of the game's increasing modernity on its traditional core values.

Cricket's Recent History of Technological Developments

It is anticipated that in the not-too-distant future, there will be a flood of technological innovations that will completely transform the game of cricket. The accuracy of decisions will be improved thanks to technological advancements such as ball-tracking systems, ultra-motion cameras, and AI-driven analytics, which will also result in a more immersive experience for both players and viewers. Additionally, the implementation of wearable technology for players could make it possible to do real-time monitoring of both their physical and mental well-being, which would result in improved player output and a decreased likelihood of injury. It is also anticipated that virtual reality (VR) and augmented reality (AR) will play a big role in improving fan engagement by bringing fans closer to the activity taking place on the field.

Possibilities for Business and Growth on a Global Scale

It is anticipated that cricket's commercial potential would skyrocket, primarily as a result of the globalization of the sport. There is a significant possibility for the sport to increase its presence around the world as new markets, like China, the United States, and other areas of Europe, are exhibiting a growing interest in cricket. This expansion will not only bring in a larger audience, but it will also bring in a huge amount of income through sponsorships, broadcasting rights, and merchandise sales. In addition, the proliferation of franchise-based leagues, such as the Indian Premier League (IPL) and the Big Bash League (BBL), will further contribute to the commercialization of the sport. These leagues will provide a stage upon which international players will be able to demonstrate their expertise and ability, resulting in the creation of a climate that is both more competitive and more financially rewarding.

The Development of Various Playing Formats and Regulations

The game of cricket will almost certainly undergo changes in its playing forms and rules in the future in order to accommodate the shifting dynamics of the modern audience. Despite the fact that the conventional Test format will continue to maintain its historical relevance, the shorter forms, such as One Day Internationals (ODIs) and Twenty20 (T20), will continue to gain additional prominence. This is due to the fact that these formats are faster-paced and more viewer-friendly than the classic Test format. The game will be made more exciting and unpredictable by the adoption of new rules, including as the usage of new cricket balls, changed fielding limits, and power plays, in order to accommodate to the preferences of a broad global audience.

Concerns Regarding Both Sustainability and the Environment

An greater focus on sustainable practices and environmental issues is certainly going to have a significant impact on cricket's future as well. It will be necessary for the sport to address challenges such as lowering its carbon footprint, conserving water, and developing environmentally friendly stadium infrastructure. Cricket will be aligned with global efforts to address climate change through the implementation of initiatives that promote green energy, waste management, and responsible water usage. These will become essential components of the sport's sustainability agenda. In addition, the use of environmentally friendly materials for cricket equipment and the encouragement of environmentally conscious behaviors among players and supporters will contribute significantly to the long-term viability of cricket as a sport.

Cricket is Dedicated to Promoting Diversity and Inclusivity

Cricket's future will be marked by a substantial push toward diversity and inclusivity, with a primary emphasis on fostering the participation of women, members of minority groups, and people hailing from communities that are underrepresented. In order to level the playing field for female cricket players, efforts are being made to close the gender gap in the sport. This will result in more women's leagues, tournaments, and grassroots programs being developed, which will create an environment that is more welcoming and equal for female players. Additionally, efforts that aim to promote cricket in non-traditional regions and communities will play a crucial part in increasing the sport's reach and cultivating a fan base that is more diverse and inclusive around the world.

Challenges to Regulatory Compliance and Concerns Regarding Integrity

Cricket's future is not without obstacles, particularly those surrounding regulatory compliance and integrity concerns, despite the fact that the company is now on a positive trajectory. The increasing prevalence of match-fixing, doping, and other forms of corruption is a huge risk to the sport's integrity and reputation. The governing bodies of Cricket will need to enforce stronger regulations, develop robust anti-corruption measures, and encourage ethical standards across all levels of the game in order to reduce the impact of these difficulties.

In the years to come, putting an emphasis on things like openness, accountability, and fair play will be essential to sustaining the spirit and integrity of the game of cricket.

Participation from Fans and Other Interactive Experiences

A paradigm shift in the way fans engage with their favorite sports will occur in the future of cricket, with a greater focus placed on interactive experiences and personalized information. Cricket fans will soon be able to have a more personal connection with their favorite teams and players thanks to the introduction of innovative digital platforms, integrations with social media, and immersive fan experiences. Fan-centric initiatives, such as virtual meet-and-greets, live question-and-answer sessions, and exclusive access behind the scenes, will deepen the emotional tie between fans and the sport, thereby cultivating a more loyal and engaged fan base across the globe.

Initiatives Focused on Grassroots Change and Youth Development

The future of cricket will be significantly influenced by the level of investment made in grassroots and youth development projects. Not only will the development of extensive training programs, the construction of state-of-the-art facilities, and the cultivation of young talent beginning at an early age result in a pool of excellent players, but it will also result in the development of a culture that values sportsmanship, discipline, and perseverance. In order to identify and cultivate future cricketing potential, collaborations between cricket boards, educational institutions, and local communities will play a critical role. These collaborations will ensure a sustained pipeline of competent players for the future.

10.1 The potential for further globalization

The economic, social, and cultural landscapes of the world have all been altered as a result of globalization, a phenomena that began to acquire steam in the latter part of the 20th century. As a result of the development of more advanced technologies, the improvement of transportation networks, and the enhancement of communication systems, the possibility for more globalization across a variety of industries has emerged as a topic that has generated a significant amount of attention and controversy. This examination digs into the various spheres of global trade, culture, technology, and governance to investigate the possibility for more globalization, its repercussions, as well as the difficulties and opportunities that it presents in the modern world.

Integration of International Commerce and the Economy

There is still a substantial amount of untapped potential for further globalization in the areas of international trade and economic integration. Countries are increasingly recognizing the benefits of open markets and global trade as a result of continued efforts to eliminate trade barriers, promote international collaboration, and expedite cross-border transactions.

The proliferation of e-commerce platforms, the rise of global supply chains, and the growth of multinational corporations have all contributed to the exchange of goods and services across international borders in a seamless manner. This has contributed to the expansion of the economy as well as the creation of new opportunities for international trade and investment.

The Promotion of Intercultural Communication and Mutual Comprehension

In the field of culture, the encouragement of cultural interchange and understanding between different cultures holds the potential for further globalization. A greater appreciation and comprehension of the world's myriad of cultural traditions and identities has resulted from increased global connectedness as well as the sharing of ideas, artistic expressions, and cultural practices. People from different regions of the world are now able to communicate with one another, share their experiences, and celebrate their cultural heritage thanks to the rise of platforms such as social media, streaming services, and international events. This has resulted in the development of a global community that is more inclusive and linked.

The advancement of technology and connectivity in the digital realm

There is a tremendous amount of room for more globalization to take place in the areas of technology innovation and digital connectivity. The seamless transmission of data, knowledge, and innovation across international borders has been made possible as a result of advancements in information technology, telecommunications, and digital infrastructure. Businesses are now able to operate on a global scale, collaborate with international partners, and leverage digital platforms to reach a wider audience as a result of the rise of artificial intelligence, blockchain technology, and the Internet of Things (IoT). This has helped fuel technological advancements and digital entrepreneurship on a global scale.

Environmental Permanence in Conjunction with International Cooperation

The possibility for further globalization resides in the collective efforts being made to address climate change, promote renewable energy, and conserve the planet's natural resources in the context of environmental sustainability and global collaboration. In order to tackle environmental concerns and advance sustainable development, international agreements such as the Paris Agreement and the United Nations Sustainable Development Goals (SDGs) have highlighted the significance of global cooperation. In order to cultivate a global ecosystem that is more robust and sustainable, it is essential to launch initiatives that promote environmentally friendly habits, green technologies, and responsible resource management.

Politics, diplomacy, and participation in multilateral forums

The promotion of diplomatic communication, international collaboration, and multilateral frameworks is crucial to the realization of the potential for greater globalization in the field of political diplomacy and multilateral engagement.

In order to cultivate a global society that is more stable, peaceful, and integrated, it is vital for states to work together to handle global difficulties such as geopolitical wars, humanitarian crises, and public health catastrophes. Platforms such as the United Nations, the World Trade Organization, and regional alliances play a vital role in the promotion of diplomatic conversation and the facilitation of constructive interaction among nations, which in turn fosters a more collaborative and inclusive approach to global governance. These platforms play a pivotal role in the promotion of diplomatic dialogue and the facilitation of constructive engagement among nations.

Both difficulties and prospects are involved

Despite the potential benefits, expanding globalization is not without its share of difficulties. There are several challenges that need to be overcome before the globe can be considered completely globalized. Some of these challenges include economic inequities, cultural homogenization, digital divisions, and geopolitical tensions. In order to address these difficulties, there needs to be a concerted effort from governments, corporations, and civil society to encourage peaceful coexistence among nations, equitable economic growth, and the preservation of cultural variety. Additionally, there needs to be a closing of the digital divide. It is possible to create a global society that is more integrated, welcoming, and prosperous by seizing the opportunities given by globalization. These opportunities include the sharing of knowledge, the diversification of economies, and the enrichment of cultures.

Implications for Both New and Developing Economies and Markets

The prospect of even greater globalization has important repercussions for developing countries and emerging markets. These regions stand to gain from an expanded access to global markets, technology breakthroughs, and foreign investments, all of which have the potential to propel economic development, generate employment opportunities, and promote sustainable growth. However, in order for these economies to effectively utilize the benefits of globalization and guarantee an equitable and sustainable growth for their inhabitants, it is very necessary for them to address challenges relating to the development of infrastructure, the enhancement of skills, and institutional changes.

The possibility for more globalization across a variety of different industries presents the global community with a wide variety of opportunities as well as challenges. Nations can jointly harness the transformative force of globalization to promote a more linked, inclusive, and sustainable world by encouraging greater economic integration, promoting cultural exchange, embracing technical innovation, and enhancing global collaboration. This can be accomplished by fostering greater economic integration, promoting cultural interchange, embracing technological innovation, and strengthening global cooperation. In order to make sure that the benefits of globalization are available to everyone and to pave the way for a more just and prosperous future on a global scale for future generations, it is vital for the many stakeholders to work together, innovate, and put sustainable development at the forefront of their priorities.

10.2 The impact of climate change on cricket

The sport of cricket, which is firmly woven in the cultural fabric of a number of different countries, is not immune to the far-reaching implications that climate change will have. The game of cricket is facing a number of problems that put its long-term viability and fundamental principles in jeopardy as a result of factors such as rising average temperatures around the world, an increase in the frequency of extreme weather events, and significant shifts in the composition of ecosystems. The purpose of this study is to conduct an in-depth investigation into the effects that climate change has had on cricket, paying particular attention to how it has affected playing conditions, infrastructure, the health and safety of players, and the overall ecology. Stakeholders can undertake preemptive efforts to prevent the harmful effects of climate change on this cherished sport if they first understand these intricate dynamics and how they interact with one another.

Alterations to the Playing Conditions as well as Interruptions Caused by the Weather

Because of climate change, playing conditions have been altered, and there have been an increased number of weather disruptions. This has had a huge impact on the scheduling and conduct of cricket matches around the world. The unpredictability of the rainfall patterns, the protracted heatwaves, and the extreme weather occurrences have caused match schedules to be altered, which has resulted in a number of delays, cancellations, and less-than-ideal playing conditions. The unpredictability of weather patterns has not only had an effect on international competitions, but it has also had an effect on domestic leagues and grassroots cricket. As a result, the opportunities for players to improve their skills and the growth of the sport at various levels have been hampered.

Implication for both the pitch and the ground conditions

The impact of climate change on cricket extends to the worsening of pitch and ground conditions. This is due to the fact that rising temperatures and shifting patterns of precipitation have had an effect on the levels of soil moisture, the behavior of pitches, and overall playing surfaces. Because of shifts in the patterns of rainfall, several places now have pitches that are drier and more abrasive, whereas other regions have seen waterlogging and increased moisture content, which has led to uneven playing surfaces and unpredictable ball behavior. The players' adaptability and skill sets have been tested as a result of these developments, which has necessitated a more complete approach to the management and upkeep of the playing field to maintain fair and consistent playing conditions.

Concerning the Health and Well-being of Players

Especially in locations that are experiencing strong heatwaves and high humidity levels, the effects of climate change can have substantial repercussions for the health and well-being of players. Players are at an increased risk of heat-related illnesses, dehydration, and physical exhaustion, all of which can have a negative influence on their ability to compete, their capacity for endurance, and their overall physical and mental well-being.

The increasing prevalence of heat stress and the associated health hazards have spurred requests for better player safety measures. These recommendations have included the establishment of heat policies, the use of cooling systems, and the supply of enough hydration as well as medical support during matches and training sessions.

Negative Effects on the Environment and the Loss of Biodiversity

The effects of climate change on cricket transcend beyond the confines of the game itself and contribute to a wider range of negative ecological effects as well as the loss of biodiversity. Alterations in temperature and rainfall patterns have caused disruptions in natural habitats, brought about changes in ecosystems, and posed a threat to the biodiversity of locations in which cricket is played. Not only has the loss of biodiversity, the reduction of green cover, and the availability of less water harmed the aesthetic appeal of cricket sites, but it has also contributed to ecological imbalances, which has decreased the overall environmental resilience and sustainability of these places.

The Obstacles Facing Infrastructure and the Adaptation Strategies Needed

The infrastructure of cricket, which includes stadiums, training facilities, and playing grounds, faces severe issues as a result of climate change. The increasing likelihood of infrastructure in cricket being damaged, deteriorating, and experiencing disruptions in its ability to function as a result of rising sea levels, intense weather events, and shifting climatic conditions. In response to these challenges, stakeholders in the cricketing community are increasingly adopting adaptation strategies, such as the use of sustainable building materials, implementation of climate-resilient designs, and the integration of eco-friendly practices, to enhance the resilience and longevity of cricket infrastructure in the face of climate change. These strategies include the use of sustainable building materials, implementation of climate-resilient designs, and the integration of eco-friendly practices.

Taking Responsibility for the Environment while Engaging in Sustainable Practices

Taking into account the effects that climate change will have on cricket, the world of sports is progressively placing an emphasis on environmentally responsible behavior and sustainable playing practices. Increasing attention has been paid to programs that encourage the use of renewable energy sources, the preservation of water supplies, the responsible management of trash, and the reduction of an individual's carbon footprint. This has resulted in a more ecologically conscious approach being taken to cricket operations and events. In order to lessen cricket's influence on the environment and foster a more sustainable and resilient future for the sport, eco-friendly stadium designs, environmentally responsible modes of transportation, and the utilization of renewable energy sources are essential components that must be implemented.

Participation in the Community and Awareness of the Climate

In order to mitigate the effects of climate change on cricket, efforts to educate the local community and raise awareness about the issue are of critical importance. In order to increase awareness about the interconnectedness between climate change, sports, and the environment, education programs, outreach efforts, and community-driven initiatives are required. Cricket stakeholders have the ability to inspire collective action, promote environmental stewardship, and contribute to the broader global efforts that are aimed at combating climate change and its adverse effects on the sporting community by cultivating a culture of climate consciousness and encouraging community participation in sustainable practices.

Interventions in Policy and Collaboration on an International Scale

In order to mitigate the myriad ways in which climate change is affecting cricket, it is essential to have effective policy interventions and widespread international cooperation. In order to produce comprehensive rules, regulations, and guidelines that prioritize climatic resilience, environmental sustainability, and player well-being, it is vital that cricketing bodies, government agencies, and environmental organizations work together. It is possible to create a more holistic approach to addressing the difficulties posed by climate change through the incorporation of climate considerations into sports governance, infrastructure planning, and event management. This will ensure the long-term viability and sustainability of cricket as a global sport.

The effects of climate change on cricket are an urgent matter that need the immediate attention and united action of the worldwide community of cricket players, administrators, and officials. Stakeholders can mitigate the negative effects of climate change on cricket by acknowledging the multifaceted challenges posed by climate change, implementing sustainable practices, fostering climate awareness, and advocating for robust policy interventions. This will ensure the resilience, sustainability, and integrity of the sport for future generations. The adoption of a preventative and comprehensive approach to climate action will not only protect the health of players and the integrity of cricketing ecosystems, but it will also contribute to the larger global efforts that are aimed at mitigating the effects of climate change and developing a sporting landscape that is more sustainable and resilient.

10.3 The evolving fan experience and technological advancements

In recent years, there has been a seismic shift in the landscape of sports fandom, mostly driven by developments in technology. This shift has been brought about by a confluence of factors. Fans of their favorite sports teams are no longer content to only watch the action unfold on the field; instead, they take an active role in the action. Not only have technological advancements improved the spectator experience, but they have also fundamentally altered the ways in which people consume, interact with, and celebrate athletic competition.

This analysis digs deeper into the ever-evolving fan experience as well as technical breakthroughs, examining the influence on a variety of sports, the rise of augmented reality (AR) and virtual reality (VR), data-driven analytics, and the potential for more fan interaction in the future.

The Impact of Recent Technological Developments on Fan Engagement

The incorporation of technology into the activities that fans participate in is quickly becoming a defining characteristic of the ever-evolving fan experience. Real-time scores, live-streamed sports, and interactive information are all easily accessible to fans thanks to the proliferation of mobile apps, social media platforms, and websites with interactive features. The level of personalization and engagement has increased as a result of the opportunity to modify content according to one's tastes and to receive notifications on one's favorite teams or players. Fans are able to instantly express their ideas with a global network of other fans, participate in live polls, and have virtual chats with other like-minded individuals.

Content Available for Live Streaming as Well as On-Demand

The introduction of live streaming and information that can be accessed on demand has brought about a sea change in the way sports fans get their sports fix. Digital platforms have supplanted traditional television broadcasts, making it possible for fans to watch games online from any location provided they have access to the internet. Streaming services provide fans with freedom, allowing them to select the watching time and device that works best for them. In addition, content that can be accessed on demand, such as highlights, interviews, and footage from behind the scenes, offers fans an all-encompassing experience that helps to cultivate a deeper connection with the sport and the players who compete in it.

Both Augmented Reality (AR) and Virtual Reality (VR) are types of mixed reality.

Fan experiences have been completely transformed as a result of the availability of immersive and interactive surroundings made possible by augmented reality (AR) and virtual reality (VR). Fans can receive real-time data, player insights, and virtual advertisements through the use of augmented reality (AR), which superimposes digital content over the real world. Fans can experience the game from the best seat in the house, attend press conferences, or engage with other fans in virtual areas if they use virtual reality (VR). VR brings fans into a 360-degree virtual arena. Augmented reality (AR) and virtual reality (VR) both increase fan engagement by giving an innovative and game-changing way to enjoy sports.

Analytics and Insights That Are Driven by Data

The availability of data-driven analytics has improved the experience of sports fans by allowing for more in-depth understanding of player performance, team plans, and game results. Fans may now get their hands on a multitude of statistical data, such as player heatmaps, shot trajectories, and in-depth game analysis.

In order to gain a more in-depth comprehension of the game, advanced measures such as Expected Goals (xG) in soccer and Player Impact Plus-Minus (PIPM) in basketball can be utilized. Fans are given the ability to participate in well-informed conversations and forecasts as a result of these analytics, which adds a level of depth to their experience.

Technology that can be worn and participation from fans

Fans are now able to take a more active role in the sports that they follow of their choice thanks to wearable technologies such as smartwatches, activity trackers, and augmented reality glasses. The availability of real-time performance data made possible by wearables enables fans to evaluate their own physical activity in relation to those of their favorite sportsmen. In other instances, students will be able to take part in virtual competitions or challenges alongside their favorite athletes, which will build a stronger feeling of connection and a sense of having shared experiences.

The use of gaming mechanics and fantasy sports

The ever-evolving fan experience now includes essential elements like gamification and fantasy sports as core components. Fans have the opportunity to participate in a variety of fantasy leagues, in which they construct virtual teams consisting of their favorite sportsmen and compete against their friends and other enthusiasts. The practice of making predictions about player performances, the results of plays, or even the next team to score is one example of how the gamification of sports has spread to in-game experiences. Fans get an additional layer of enjoyment and a chance to compete thanks to these interactive components, which keep them interested in the game from beginning to end.

Fan communities all across the world and social media

Platforms for social media have made it easier for people all over the world to build fan communities for their favorite artists and musicians, overcoming both physical and cultural barriers. Fans can make connections with other fans all across the world, talk about what they're passionate about, and take part in conversations that span several languages and time zones. Platforms such as Twitter, Facebook, and Instagram have become hotspots for user-generated material, allowing followers to express their devotion and creativity through memes, videos, and fan art. This content may be found on these platforms.

Experience That Fans Get During Live Events

The evolution of the fan experience at live events has occurred concurrently with the substantial technology advances that have been made in remote fan engagement. The use of cutting-edge technology in stadiums and arenas has recently become commonplace in order to improve the fan experience. Even if they are physically present at the game, spectators are nevertheless able to remain linked to the digital world thanks to the presence of giant LED screens, interactive kiosks, and high-speed Wi-Fi.

Attending live events is made more convenient and secure by the use of technologies such as augmented reality apps, mobile ticketing systems, and cashless payment methods.

Confrontations, as well as Ethical Considerations

The ever-evolving fan experience made possible by technology presents both obstacles and opportunities for ethical reflection, notwithstanding the many benefits that it confers. There are a number of issues that require careful consideration, including worries about privacy in connection with data collecting, the potential for addiction to sports-related gambling and fantasy leagues, and the possibility of misinformation spreading on social media. It is still very important for sports organizations and technology suppliers to strike a healthy balance between fan involvement and appropriate and ethical business operations.

The Path Forward for Participation from Fans

The landscape of future fan engagement is one that is constantly shifting, and there are fresh technology advances on the horizon. The implementation of artificial intelligence (AI) for the purpose of making personalized content recommendations, the extension of blockchain technology for the purpose of making fan participation more secure and transparent, and future breakthroughs in augmented reality and virtual reality experiences are all potential developments. Fan engagement may also extend beyond traditional sports, including virtual sports, esports, and sports that utilize developing technologies such as drone racing and virtual reality competitions.

The ever-evolving fan experience, which is being driven by technological improvements, has turned the journey of being a sports fan into one that is dynamic and engaging. Fans now have access to an abundance of information, the capacity to participate in fully immersive virtual settings, and a sense of belonging to a worldwide community that is not restricted by national boundaries. Although the technology has, in many ways, improved the fan experience, it has also introduced new concerns that need for awareness and the consideration of ethical issues. The future of fan interaction contains even more intriguing possibilities, offering a landscape where sports fans can enjoy a more personalized, immersive, and participatory experience that transcends the bounds of time and location. The future of fan engagement holds even more exciting possibilities. The world of sports must remain flexible and learn to harness the power of innovation as technology continues to improve in order to fulfill the ever-shifting requirements and requirements of spectators.